BEST PRACTICES IN PREVENTION

Other Books in the Prevention Practice Kit

Sally Hage: *To Evan who brings such joy and laughter to my life*
John Romano: *To Mom and Dad who taught empathy
for others and the importance of learning*

BEST PRACTICES IN PREVENTION

SALLY HAGE
University of Albany

JOHN L. ROMANO
University of Minnesota

Los Angeles | London | New Delhi
Singapore | Washington DC

Los Angeles | London | New Delhi
Singapore | Washington DC

FOR INFORMATION:

SAGE Publications, Inc.
2455 Teller Road
Thousand Oaks, California 91320
E-mail: order@sagepub.com

SAGE Publications Ltd.
1 Oliver's Yard
55 City Road
London EC1Y 1SP
United Kingdom

SAGE Publications India Pvt. Ltd.
B 1/I 1 Mohan Cooperative Industrial Area
Mathura Road, New Delhi 110 044
India

SAGE Publications Asia-Pacific Pte. Ltd.
3 Church Street
#10-04 Samsung Hub
Singapore 049483

Acquisitions Editor: Kassie Graves
Editorial Assistant: Elizabeth Luizzi
Production Editor: Brittany Bauhaus
Copy Editor: QuADS Prepress (P) Ltd.
Typesetter: C&M Digitals (P) Ltd.
Proofreader: Jeff Bryant
Indexer: Diggs Publication Services, Inc.
Cover Designer: Glenn Vogel
Marketing Manager: Lisa Sheldon Brown
Permissions Editor: Adele Hutchinson

Copyright © 2013 by SAGE Publications, Inc.

Printed in the United States of America

Library of Congress Cataloging-in-Publication Data

Best practices in prevention / editors, Sally Hage, John L. Romano.

p. cm. — (Prevention practice kit)
Includes bibliographical references and index.

ISBN 978-1-4522-5797-6 (pbk.)

1. Preventive mental health services—Standards.
2. Health promotion—Standards. I. Hage, Sally.
II. Romano, John L.

RA790.B4395 2013
362.1—dc23   2012040370

This book is printed on acid-free paper.

12 13 14 15 16 10 9 8 7 6 5 4 3 2 1

Brief Contents _____

Detailed Contents _____

Acknowledgments_____

We would like to thank our graduate students who provided invaluable assistance on prevention projects through literature reviews, insightful discussions, and research applications.

1

Why Practice Prevention? Why Now?

Prevention is better than cure.

—Desiderius Erasmus (n.d.)

Erasmus may have been a classical scholar during the Reformation, more than 500 years ago, but he shared a bit of wisdom during this period—that it is better to prevent illness than to cure it—that is now beginning to take a much stronger hold, especially in the helping professions. A movement from a focus on curing illness after it has begun to *actually* preventing it before it emerges is underway in the United States. One indicator of this shift was the release of the *National Prevention Strategy* (National Prevention Council, 2011) on June 16, 2011, by members of the Obama administration, led by members of the National Prevention, Health Promotion, and Public Health Council. This plan aims to improve the health and well-being of Americans and to weave prevention into all aspects of our lives, including quality medical care, clean air and water, safe outdoor spaces for physical activity, safe work sites, healthy foods, violence-free environments, and healthy homes. The release of this *Strategy* is one of several indicators of a paradigm shift taking place in the United States, pointing to a change from a system focused on the treatment of disease to one that also promotes health and wellness.

The American public, along with government leaders, is voicing the need to place prevention initiatives in the forefront of major health care priorities. For example, a recent poll indicated that 71% of Americans favor increasing investment in disease prevention and making prevention a top priority in future health reform (Trust for America's Health, 2009). In addition, legislative reform of the health care system increasingly mandates inclusion of prevention services as an important component of overall health care. The Patient Protection and Affordable Care Act, United States health care legislation signed by President Obama in 2010, makes wellness and prevention services accessible by requiring health plans to cover prevention services without co-pays. These services include counseling to promote a healthier lifestyle (e.g., proper nutrition, weight management) and to reduce depression and well-baby prevention services (www.healthcare.gov/law/aboutprovisions/services/index.html).

Focus of This Book

This book in the *Prevention Practice Kit* will detail practical steps that need to be considered by prevention practitioners as they engage with others in developing and delivering prevention projects. A context for engaging in prevention practice will be provided, including factors pointing toward an increased focus on prevention, how prevention fits in with traditional models of psychology, and popular theoretical models for doing prevention practice. The reader will learn about the *Guidelines for Prevention Practice, Research, and Education* (manuscript in preparation) and why these aspirational standards are important to consider. The book will also highlight the essential aspects of collaboration, cultural relevance and social justice, and program dissemination and attend to often knotty ethical issues surrounding confidentiality in prevention and health promotion efforts. Finally, to help readers apply what they learn, examples and activities are sprinkled throughout the book accompanied by a set of learning exercises.

Factors Accounting for Shift to Prevention

At least two circumstances appear to account for the movement toward a prevention focus. The first one is an increased awareness of the staggering financial cost of the current health care system, particularly relative to the recent economic downturn. Health care spending in the United States is approaching $2 trillion a year and is expected to double in the next 10 years. As noted by President Obama, "In the absence of a radical shift towards prevention and public health, we will not be successful in containing medical costs or improving the health of the American people" (Trust for America's Health, 2009). Increasing evidence suggests prevention makes financial sense. For example, a review of health promotion programs found a significant return on investment for these programs, with benefit-to-cost ratios ranging from $1.49 to $4.91 (median of $3.14) in benefits for every dollar spent on the program (U.S. Department of Health and Human Services, 2003).

The second factor moving the U.S. system toward prevention is increased awareness of research, indicating that negative health behaviors (e.g., smoking, poor diet, lack of exercise, and excessive alcohol) account for at least 50% of all chronic health problems and 40% of premature deaths in the United States (National Center for Chronic Disease Prevention and Health Promotion, 2009). These conditions include heart disease, diabetes, asthma, and obesity. Chronic health conditions are projected to become the leading cause of disability globally by the year 2020; if not successfully prevented, they will become the most expensive problems faced by health care systems worldwide (World Health Organization, 2011). Hence, prevention efforts increasingly target individual behavior and lifestyle choices that influence the development and course of these chronic conditions.

Furthermore, evidence increasingly suggests that mental illness, such as depression, is inexorably linked with chronic health problems, such as cardio-vascular disease and diabetes (Vogelzang et al., 2008). This link between physical well-being and mental health requires health professionals to work more closely in implementing health promotion strategies. In addition, evidence is growing that mental health symptoms and issues are interrelated with other problems of youths, such as drug use, delinquency, and school failure (Mrazek, Biglan, & Hawkins, 2004). Hence, the leadership of psychologists and other mental health professionals is critical in the implementation of a prevention focus in our health care system.

It is also crucial that efforts by prevention practitioners and others focus the mental health field toward prevention to extend across the life span, beginning when children are very young and continuing into older age. For example, it is estimated that from birth, between 9% and 20% of children experience social and emotional problems that negatively affect their functioning and development (Brauner & Stephen, 2006; Costello et al., 1996), whereas studies suggest that current services meet the needs of only 13% of minority group children and 31% of nonminority children (Ringel & Sturm, 2001). Additionally, while people of age 65 and older constitute only 12% of the U.S. population, they account for 16% of suicide deaths (Centers for Disease Control and Prevention, National Center for Injury Prevention and Control, 2005). Furthermore, the majority of older adults who die by suicide—up to 75%—report visiting a physician during the 1-month period before death (Conwell, 2001).

How Does Prevention Fit With Traditional Models of Psychology?

Traditional psychology often focuses on defining a problem within an individual and then finds ways to treat the problem using various techniques. Frequently, a mental health professional will explore the past and present behaviors of an individual and any traumatic events that may have occurred during the person's life and how these events have contributed to the overall functioning of the individual. The provider will then choose an appropriate treatment method to assist with resolving the problem or concern and enhance future behaviors. Increasingly these treatment approaches are evidence-based therapies, such as cognitive behavioral therapy. While treatments for mental health problems have made great strides over the past two decades, the problem is that these emerging evidence-based therapies are not getting to the people who need them. Nearly 50% of the American population suffers some kind of mental illness at least once in their lifetime, but the field of psychology, which relies largely on individual psychotherapy to treat those in need of care, lacks the resources to help the vast majority of those who need care. The overwhelming majority, some 70%, currently are not helped (Kazdin & Blase, 2011).

Therefore, the aim of psychotherapy, unlike prevention, is to treat an individual *after* he or she has a disorder or disease rather than to *prevent* it from occurring in the first place. Also, treatment, such as psychotherapy, is not the same as prevention as it does not reduce the incidence rate of mental illness. Primary prevention, on the other hand, attempts to reduce incidence rates of mental disorders and distress in groups of people rather than in individuals as psychotherapy does. Furthermore, for prevention efforts to be effective, intervention and education needs to happen across multiple contexts, including, but also beyond, the traditional psychotherapy relationship. Psychologists need to utilize client interactions as opportunities for prevention, but they also need to be involved in prevention programming and policy initiatives within the contexts of communities, schools, and governments.

Prevention calls for new types of roles that practitioners have begun to assume, and preparation for these new roles requires the development of new models of training, practice, research, and social advocacy (Hage et al., 2007). As noted by the 2009 APA Presidential Task Force on the Future of Psychology Practice, a "major overhaul" of psychology's training programs is needed to prepare psychologists for "the new world psychology finds itself in" (Martin, 2009, p. 66). Therefore, it is important for psychologists and other mental health professionals to gain the knowledge and skills needed to engage with individuals, families, and their communities in health promotion and disease prevention strategies (World Health Organization, 2011).

Prevention, like every major scientific field, is dominated by a handful of foundational theories. These theories guide research, practice, curriculum development, and evaluation and help develop effective instructional tactics and strategies. In the next section, you will be introduced to several of these theoretical and conceptual models, which form the foundation of a prevention approach.

Theoretical and Conceptual Models for Prevention

The science and practice of prevention have evolved across several disciplines, including psychology, counseling, education, public health, and social work. One of the strengths of the scholarship of prevention is that these and other disciplines have contributed to its development in the 20th and 21st centuries. Contributions have come from many sources, including the development of settlement houses and the mental health movement from the beginning of the 20th century to the mid-1960s and the introduction of the specialty of community psychology and into the 21st century, when prevention has received increased attention in the counseling and psychology professions, and attended to in federal policy initiatives (e.g., United States federal health care legislation). This strength, however, has also been a limitation, primarily because different disciplines have not historically collaborated on prevention interventions, research, and training. We believe, however, that the lack of collaboration across disciplines is slowly changing, as universities and training programs are emphasizing interdisciplinary scholarship among faculty and students, and the science of prevention lends itself nicely to interdisciplinary collaboration.

One notable example is the Prevention Science Graduate Minor at the University of Minnesota, which is an interdisciplinary graduate-level minor with participation of students and faculty from many departments across the university, including education, family social science, kinesiology, nursing, psychiatry, psychology, public health, public policy, and social work. The importance of interdisciplinary work is further supported as funding agencies are increasingly demanding that prevention research and intervention proposals be supported by multidisciplinary teams of scholars and practitioners. As Romano (2013) has written, interdisciplinary collaborations between prevention specialists and specialists from other disciplines will be increasingly necessary in the 21st century. Romano specifically writes about psychologists and other human development professionals collaborating with specialists in areas such as neuroscience, genetics, applied economics, public policy, and information technology. Romano predicts that these areas are increasingly important in prevention research and practice, and these are areas not traditionally taught with any depth in applied psychology, counseling, social work, and other human development training programs. Therefore, collaborations with professionals across disciplines are extremely important.

At least partially due to the lack of multidisciplinary collaboration in prevention training, practice, and research, theoretical conceptualizations and perspectives to support prevention interventions have often been lacking. The most popular theories taught in various disciplines may not be applicable to prevention interventions, or they are not taught with a prevention application. An example of the former from counseling psychology is person-centered theory, while cognitive behavioral theory is an example of the latter. Therefore, too often, prevention interventions are delivered without a sound theoretical basis. For example, Painter, Borba, Hynes, Mays, and Glanz (2008) reviewed literature from 2000 to 2005 in health behavior research and found that only about one third of the empirical studies used a theoretical framework; furthermore, the lack of theory-based interventions had not changed significantly since an earlier review of research conducted in the 1990s.

In addition, others have written about uncoordinated and fragmented school-based prevention interventions (Greenberg et al., 2003). Partially, as a result, school-based prevention interventions have lacked an articulated theoretical foundation and, often, have been driven by national and community crises that spurred increased federal legislation and funding opportunities. For example, in the late 1980s, after the cocaine-induced death of a highly recruited University of Maryland professional basketball prospect, Len Bias, stronger federal antidrug legislation was enacted, including a federal office and grants program for "drug-free schools," under the U.S. Department of Education. Within a few years, to prevent school and community violence, the Safe and Drug-Free Schools and Communities Act was passed during President Clinton's administration. More recently, school-based bullying has prompted state legislatures to enact antibullying and harassment laws.

Activity

Select a prevention program in your community or work place, and after reviewing the program, identify the theory or perspective that serves as foundation to the program.

2 Four Theories and Perspectives to Support Prevention Interventions

I n this chapter, four theoretical frameworks or perspectives that may form a theoretical foundation for prevention interventions are summarized. They are (1) transtheoretical model of behavior change (TTM), (2) theory of reasoned action and planned behavior (TRA/PB), (3) positive psychology, and (4) social justice. The first two are considered theories in the traditional understanding of theory, while the latter two are more broad-based perspectives that may inform prevention work. These theories and perspectives were chosen as they have many applications in prevention research and interventions. Also, they are not regularly taught in many training programs, especially in counseling and applied psychology programs, where the emphasis is on theories that support remediation interventions.

Transtheoretical Model of Behavior Change

TTM is a well-researched theory that has been used widely to understand the change process across many different types of problem behaviors to improve physical and mental health (Prochaska, Johnson, & Lee, 2009). Initially, TTM was developed to understand how people make changes to reduce addictive behaviors (e.g., cigarette smoking, alcohol use; Prochaska, DiClemente, & Norcross, 1992). TTM was conceptualized after reviews of different theories of psychotherapy revealed relatively few processes across the major theories of psychotherapy and behavior change that bring about change (Prochaska et al., 2009)—therefore, the term, *transtheoretical*, in the title of TTM. TTM is referred to as a stage theory of change, as its originators believe that people make behavioral changes as a result of progressing through a series of stages, but not necessarily in linear progression.

According to TTM, behavioral change occurs as a process over six stages: (1) precontemplation, (2) contemplation, (3) preparation, (4) action, (5) maintenance, and (6) termination (Prochaska et al., 2009). In the *precontemplation* stage, people are not intending to make changes in the near future (within the next 6 months), and they may not even be aware that change is important or necessary to their health and well-being. During the *contemplation* stage, people are intending to take action to change their behavior within 6 months. They recognize that change is necessary and realize the advantages and disadvantages of making the change. During the *preparation* stage, people plan to take action to bring about change within the next month and have typically taken some action to initiate the change. For example, they may have consulted with a health professional or become self-educated about the behavior. In the *action* stage, people have made modifications to their behavior to implement the behavioral change. In TTM, behavior change must be observable and recorded, such as the number of cigarettes smoked each day or body weight measured weekly; behavioral changes are measured so as to be empirically analyzed. The next stage, *maintenance*, focuses on relapse prevention, or maintaining the behavioral changes made during the action stage. Normally, this stage lasts up to 5 years but, in reality, may last a lifetime, for example, abstaining from smoking or maintaining ideal body weight. The final stage, *termination*, refers to people who are completely free of temptation of returning to the problem behavior. In reality, this TTM stage is rare, and this stage has not received much research attention (Prochaska et al., 2009).

TTM is an important framework to consider when designing prevention interventions. The theory explicitly emphasizes that all recipients of a prevention intervention are not likely to be at the same readiness for change stage. Therefore, applying the same prevention intervention across an entire sample or population group may meet with limited success, as all members of the group will not be at the same stage of readiness for change. Prevention interventions, even more so than traditional counseling interventions where clients are often self-referred, usually are delivered across a particular segment of the population, community, or institution. For example, all middle school students may receive a bully prevention program, or work settings may offer a heart healthy cafeteria menu. TTM offers a strong recommendation that prevention specialists assess readiness for change of the population before a prevention program is implemented. It may be that different aspects of the prevention intervention are delivered to different subsets of the sample, depending on their stage of readiness for change. Of course, this step would require an assessment of the readiness for change of the sample prior to the implementation of an intervention. Prevention programs generally assume that all recipients of the intervention are at the same stage of readiness for change; and, even more specifically, many prevention programs assume that recipients are at the action stage of change. Therefore, in the planning stages, it is recommended that prevention specialists assess the stage of readiness for change of the group receiving the prevention intervention. This could be achieved through one or more of the following: focus groups with potential recipients of the prevention intervention, needs assessment surveys of potential recipients, and discussions with major stakeholders apart from the recipients, for example, community leaders, parents, and teachers. Assessing readiness for change can strengthen the prevention intervention, but it may also require that prevention specialists adapt parts of a prevention program to meet the stage of readiness of different recipients.

An innovative example based on TTM theory of an individualized, short-term, computer-generated expert system to deliver a school-based bullying prevention program was described by Prochaska, Evers, Prochaska, Van Marter, and Johnson (2007). The intervention was designed to give guidance and instructions to individuals based on their readiness for change related to bullying behaviors as aggressor, victim, or bystander. The computer program delivered to each student provides a tailored intervention based on the student's readiness for change, which was assessed at pretest. The results from this prevention intervention trial, delivered to nearly 2,500 middle and high school students across the United States, showed that students in the treatment groups were more likely to progress to the action stage of change compared with control groups and that the treatment students were less likely to participate in any of the three bullying behaviors (aggressor, victim, bystander) compared with controls. This is an excellent example of how TTM theory might be used to individualize prevention interventions for large samples and match the level of intervention to each person's readiness for change. While such technological interventions are costly and complex to develop, implementation is much less costly in terms of staff time and material resources compared with more traditional prevention interventions.

Activity

Examine lifestyle behaviors that you would like to change. What stage of readiness for change, based on TTM theory, are you at with each behavior?

Theory of Reasoned Action and Planned Behavior

TRA/PB has received much attention in social psychology research but less so in applied areas of psychology, including in prevention applications. TRA was first proposed by Fishbein (1967) to explain the relationship between a person's attitudes, beliefs, and behaviors that are under the person's control. TRA makes an important differentiation between an attitude toward an object and an attitude toward a behavior related to that object (Montaño & Kasprzky, 2002). For example, a person may have negative attitudes about developing diabetes (object) but less negative attitudes about changing eating and exercise behaviors (behavior) that place the person at risk for diabetes. According to TRA, attitudes toward behaviors are strong predictors of behavior change. However, since not all behavior is under complete voluntary control of individuals, Ajzen (1991) proposed that perceived behavioral control (PBC), from the theory of PB, be added to TRA. PBC refers to a person's belief about the extent that a behavior is under his or her control. Thus, PBC is related to Bandura's (1986) theory of self-efficacy. Thus, TRA/ PB is expressed as follows: Behavior is a function of intentions to carry out a behavior, while intentions are a function of a person's attitudes, social norms, and PBC [symbolically expressed as *Behavior* $\approx$ *Intentions* $\approx$ *(Attitudes + Norms + Control)*]. In this conceptualization, social norms refer to a person's beliefs about what other people important to the person think is appropriate behavior and the person's willingness to adhere to the opinions of others. Important people may be parents, guardians, teachers, peers, coaches, partners, or whoever is significant in the person's life.

Because attitudes, social norms, and PBC can vary widely across population groups, depending on any number of variables such as gender, age, ethnic group, socioeconomic class, and so on, a procedure called elicitation research has been used with TRA/PB. Elicitation research assesses TRA/PB variables of attitudes, norms, and behavioral control that are most salient to those who will receive the prevention intervention. Elicitation research is completed prior to delivering the intervention; and most important, elicitation research will then help the prevention specialist refine the prevention intervention specifically for those who will receive it. Through elicitation research, prevention specialists can assess the most important variables of the group that will receive the prevention intervention and then construct the intervention accordingly. Elicitation research is especially important for prevention specialists who intervene with population groups with whom they have little identity or knowledge. Romano and Netland (2008) present examples of elicitation research in their review of TRA/PB. An excellent resource by Ajzen is available to assist practitioners and researchers who wish to develop TRA/PB measures and procedures (http://www.people.umass.edu/ aizen/tpb.html). Also, consult Fishbein and Ajzen (2010) for additional assistance when developing TRA/PB questionnaires.

TRA/PB is a model that addresses the most salient attitudes and beliefs that motivate people to either remain with present behaviors or adapt new and more health-enhancing behaviors. The theory proposes that behaviors are influenced by intentions to change behaviors, and intentions are related to (a) attitudes about the behaviors, (b) how people important to the subject group view the behaviors, and (c) the amount of control that the members of the subject group believe that they have over the behaviors. Therefore, measuring the subject groups' attitudes, social norms, and perceived control prior to developing the prevention intervention will provide information so that the prevention intervention can address components of the most important variables that may motivate group members to change behaviors. For example, in developing a high school alcohol prevention program, it is important to assess through elicitation research the attitudes of different groups in the school toward alcohol use. Girls will likely have attitudes different from boys about drinking; they may have different beliefs about the attitudes of people important to them about drinking; and they may have different beliefs about their control over drinking. Similar differences may be found among different grade levels or socioeconomic groups. In this high school example, male and female athletes may be more influenced not to use alcohol because it could result in being dropped from athletic teams, and they will more strongly receive disapproval from coaches (social norm). Other student groups may believe that unless they use alcohol, they will be less popular with their peers (social norms) and, thus, perceive themselves as having less control in their use of alcohol (PBC). Therefore, by being aware of these and other influences during the development of a prevention intervention, the prevention specialist will be better able to address the influences that are most salient to the target group.

While TRA/PB has been used as foundation for different prevention interventions, the model has often been incorrectly applied, and much of the research has focused on variables that address behavioral intentions (Romano & Netland, 2008). While Ajzen and Fishbein (2004) believe that behavioral intentions can serve as a substitute for assessing actual behavior change when it is not practical or ethical to assess behavior change, the most important consideration to determine success of a prevention intervention is whether or not the intervention results in behavior change. Therefore, it is important to assess actual behavior change after a TRA/PB-based prevention intervention has been implemented. For example, Montaño and Kasprzky (2002) in their study of women at risk for HIV infection reported that after assessing intentions to use condoms, the researchers followed up with participants 3 months later and asked about actual condom use. In this study, intention to use condoms was highly correlated with condom use 3 months later.

In an application of TRA and persuasive messages, Christopher, Skillman, Kirkhart, and D'Souza (2006) investigated professional help-seeking behavior among undergraduate college students, comparing students in the United States with Thai students studying at a university in Bangkok. Elicitation research was used during the first phase of the study to assess student beliefs about the advantages and disadvantages of seeking psychological professional help (i.e., attitudes) and how people important to the students would perceive the students' decision to seek psychological help (i.e., subject norms). Data gathered from this first phase was used in Phase 2 of the research with undergraduate students different from those who participated in the first phase. Participants in Phase 2 read the same description of professional psychological help given to students in Phase 1, but it was followed by an additional persuasive message based on beliefs and norms elicited in Phase 1 from U.S. and Thai students. Intention to seek psychological help was measured with a single item. The authors found that information about psychological services provided to students from different cultures makes a difference in students' intentions to use psychological services. The authors did not assess PBC in this study, and PBC may have influenced the results, especially if students were not aware of psychological services on campus. However, this study showed that the advertisement of counseling services on college campuses can be enhanced if information disseminated about the services considers the attitudes, beliefs, and subjective norms of different student groups who may use the services. This is especially important if the services are underutilized by subgroups of students on campus (e.g., international students).

The theory of TRA/PB with elicitation research is useful during the development and implementation of prevention programs across multiple contexts. In a middle school setting, for example, school counselors might use the theory and elicitation research to develop a program to promote healthy eating and prevent obesity by assessing student intentions and attitudes, social norms, and students' perceived control related to healthy nutrition and weight. Beginning with elicitation research with subgroups of students, school counselors meet with groups of students to assess their attitudes, social norms, and perceived control about food and exercise. To begin, school counselors meet in small groups with subgroups of middle school girls and boys, representing different student demographics, for example, different ethnic and socioeconomic groups, asking them about their beliefs (attitudes) about food and physical exercise: "What do you think about your overall food diet and the amount of physical exercise you get?" "How does a person's weight and diet affect them in their life?" "Would you like to change the type of food you eat and the amount of exercise you get, why or why not?" Next the counselors can inquire about how others important to the students think about their diet and exercise activities: "What do your parents think about your diet and physical exercise activities?" "Do your friends ever comment on your food or weight?" "Do you eat and exercise because of participation in sports?" Next, students can be asked about how much control they believe that they have about eating and exercise: "What do you know about the relationship between good nutrition and physical exercise?" "How much control do you have over the food you eat and your exercise activity?" "What consequences might there be if you do not eat well and exercise?" These are only sample questions and one approach. School counselors could also gather information through questionnaires, which have the advantage of being anonymous and requiring less counselor time. The questionnaires can also ask for demographic information germane to the topic, for example, sex, age, ethnic group, and so on. Once elicitation research information is reviewed, counselors can develop a health promotion program that addresses the most important variables to subgroups of students. For example, seventh-grade girls may have very different attitudes and beliefs about healthy eating and exercise compared with seventh-grade boys. Or students from ethnic minority groups may have different beliefs about the amount of control they have over changing eating and exercise habits compared with majority group students. The TRA/PB model stresses that differences within the population sample are important to identify prior to developing a prevention program, so that the prevention specialist can incorporate these differences within an overall prevention program about the topic or develop a program more specifically for students most at risk for developing problems. Thus, TRA/PB argues against a "one-size-fits-all" approach. In the example just described, it may be unrealistic for school counselors to develop several different programs on the same topic for subgroups of students. However, differences can be addressed throughout the program through examples, activities, and written handouts. However, the school counselor must be aware of the differences. Thus, students are more likely to accept the relevance of the prevention program, given their own context. Once the prevention program is implemented and completed, students can be followed to assess if the program was successful in changing student attitudes, norms, and control beliefs about a healthy diet and exercise and, most important, whether behavioral changes were actually made.

Activity

Conduct a pilot elicitation interview with two people who are different in some demographic characteristic (e.g., gender, sexual orientation, race, etc.). Ask them about their attitudes toward a behavior that they want to change (what will motivate them to change the behavior and deterrents to changing the behavior), what important people around them believe about the behavior they wish to change, and the extent of their control to change the behavior. What differences did you find between the two people, and how might you address the differences in a prevention intervention?

Positive Psychology

Positive psychology, as a perspective of psychological research and application, has received much interest during the latter years of the past century and during the early years of the 21st century. Snyder and Lopez (2007) describe positive psychology as both a scientific and applied approach that identifies individual strengths and promotes positive human functioning. Seligman, Steen, Park, and Peterson (2005) broaden the definition beyond individuals to include the promotion of positive characteristics within institutions such as schools and work places. The growth of the positive psychology movement has been impressive, as it has spurred specialized journals, book length volumes, conferences, training programs, and Internet-based information and education (Lopez, & Snyder, 2009; Seligman et al., 2005).

A positive psychology perspective fits nicely into a prevention framework, as positive psychology studies and promotes individual, group, and institutional assets, and draws attention to what is right with people as opposed to what is wrong. Historically, an emphasis on positive human functioning has been lacking in psychological training, research, and applications for a long time.

Positive psychology emphasizes the promotion and study of positive human and institutional characteristics that can serve as protections against dysfunctional behaviors. While other theoretical frameworks focus on the prevention of problem behaviors, such as drug use, depression, and interpersonal violence, positive psychology studies the promotion of positive behaviors that can serve as protective factors against problem and dysfunctional behaviors, such as individual, group, and institutional strengths and assets. For example, resiliency has been described as a characteristic of children and adolescents who, despite being raised in adverse and risk situations, manage to avoid major problem behaviors and dysfunctional lifestyles as they develop into adolescents and young adults (Masten, Best, & Garmezy, 1990; Werner & Smith, 1992).

Several characteristics have been attributed to the development of resiliency in youth, including individual and environmental factors, such as caring adults in the child's social environment (Luthar, Cicchetti, & Becker, 2000). Therefore, as an example, one potential protective factor for children at risk for problem behaviors is the opportunity for children to be supported by a mentoring relationship with a caring adult. The adult could be a parent, teacher, coach, relative, spiritual director, or anyone who takes a personal and sustained interest in the child and provides time and guidance to the child. This idea is not new as many communities have had programs for many years, such as Big Brother and Big Sister, to provide adult mentoring and friendship to children in need. Colleges and universities as well as corporations and other societal institutions have also initiated similar adult mentoring programs for youth living in adverse situations.

Within a prevention and health promotion framework, positive psychology addresses and encourages the development of characteristics and assets that can serve as protective factors against problem behaviors. Development of individual characteristics and assets as protections for youth have been disseminated since the 1990s through the Search Institute in Minneapolis, Minnesota (www.search-institute.org). The Search Institute's comprehensive analyses of data collected from youth throughout the United States identified 40 developmental assets, 20 of which are internal to youth and 20 are external. Internal assets are characteristics such as motivation to achieve, caring for others, and self-esteem. External assets include living in supportive and caring social environments, creative and healthy use of leisure time, and the amount and quality of community resources and services available to youth (Snyder & Lopez, 2007). The Search Institute publishes many products to assist youth and communities increase and strengthen youth assets. These products include books and research papers as well as training programs for school personnel, community caregivers, and community leaders. The importance of research is demonstrated through products that help institutions and communities measure assets and deficits of youth. The Search Institute promotes the importance of total community involvement to develop youth assets, as made popular by the proverb *It takes a whole village to raise a child* (Benson, 2006).

In one study of developmental assets conducted with at-risk female and male middle and junior high school students who were referred to a residential juvenile justice center, not surprisingly it was found that most students lacked protective factors in several internal and external areas (Chew, Osseck, Raygor, Eldridge-Houser, & Cox, 2010). Assets were assessed with the *Developmental Assets Profile* (DAP; Search Institute). Most of these youth lacked positive peer and parental influences and support and scored low on involvement in religious and community service activities. The students also reported difficulties with substance abuse. The students surveyed with the DAP were already experiencing problem and risk behaviors. However, as the authors suggest, school–community partnerships that support developmental assets in youth can help reduce youth risk behaviors and their involvement with the juvenile justice system, while improving the youth's overall health. Assessing development assets can help prevention specialists and school personnel, for example, identify the lack of youth protective factors in a given school or community and work to implement prevention programs that strengthen youth developmental assets.

In another example of an application of developmental assets, the Cub Scouts have shown how scouting supports and enhances the developmental assets of elementary school youth. For example, scouting can strengthen family relationships as measured by involvement of parents in a child's scouting activities. Scouting can help empower youth and enhance communities through community service projects, such as collecting items for food shelves and improving the environment through community recycling programs. Personal values such as honesty, integrity, and working for equality and social justice are also assets that are strongly enriched through scouting (www .scouting.org/About/Research/search_inst.aspx).

Another school-based resource, emphasizing developmental assets of youth to prevent bullying in the elementary school, was developed by Horne, Bartolomucci, and Newman (2003). This excellent resource is a manual for elementary school teachers to assist them in teaching developmentally appropriate skills to prevent bullying problems. The manual incorporates material related to bullies, victims, and bystanders and emphasizes developmental assets as a core component of skills training for young students.

In addition to assessments and materials developed by the Search Institute, other researchers have developed materials and measures to assess individual strengths of youth and adults. One measure, *StrengthsFinder*, is a web-based assessment (www.strengthsfinder.com) designed to assess individual characteristics and values, such as achievement motivation, defining one's purpose in life, staying on track and following through, being enthusiastic, and taking responsibility for one's activities.

Interventions that develop and strengthen positive attitudes, behaviors, and skills that promote health-enhancing behaviors (in the broadest use of the word *health*, including physical, emotional, and relational health) are critically important in prevention. Positive psychology provides a framework on which to base interventions that promote individual and group assets and strengths as protections against problematic, dysfunctional, and addictive behaviors. Prevention specialists are encouraged to assess the assets and deficits of individuals and groups with whom they work, so that the development of assets as protective characteristics can become major components of any prevention intervention. For example, in a community of adolescents who believe that alcohol use is the major leisure activity of their peers during a weekend, adolescents can be taught health-enhancing leisure behaviors and dispel the myth (which it usually is) that "most kids" are drinking on Saturday night. Younger children can be taught how to make sound decisions and form healthy peer relationships. These are only a few examples of how the focus of a prevention intervention can emphasize protection by teaching positive attitudes, behaviors, and skills to prevent future dysfunctional behaviors.

At a community, neighborhood, or institutional level, positive psychology can also form the foundation for interventions that teach health-enhancing behaviors, such as serving healthy food in school lunch rooms, providing vending machines, and supporting local facilities and resources to engage children and adolescents in healthy recreational activities, especially when school is not in session. Community resources, such as sporting facilities, libraries, and family nights at recreation centers can enhance the entire community, as well as promote positive behaviors in youth and families.

The positive psychology framework provides a large umbrella under which prevention specialists can anchor their interventions and research and help promote developmentally appropriate assets of individuals, groups (e.g., family), and institutions (e.g., schools) as protections and, thus, reduce the risk of serious problems in the future.

Activity

Design a health-enhancing prevention intervention that emphasizes the development of protective factors or positive characteristics of a group with whom you work. State why these characteristics are important and how they will serve as protections for your group.

Social Justice

It is important that prevention specialists be mindful of social justice considerations in the development of prevention interventions, programs, and research. George Albee (1959, 1986, 2005) was an early and longtime advocate for the necessity of psychology to address issues of social justice, and Albee was a particularly influential leader in promoting a social justice perspective within a prevention framework (Albee, 1999, 2000).

A social justice perspective in prevention is important because a social justice perspective adheres to the belief that many of the ills, difficulties, and problems of members of society are due to injustices that permeate across the socioeconomic landscape of a given community and the larger society. A social justice perspective holds that the least powerful members of society—those with the fewest economic and social resources and those who experience discrimination—are more likely to be victimized, to experience physical and psychological problems, and to be disadvantaged with respect to opportunities compared with more privileged members of society. Current examples in the United States include health and educational disparities among ethnic minority groups compared with members of the majority culture. A social justice perspective within prevention not only focuses on individuals and small groups but also attempts to change larger societal injustices that create environments that lead to disempowerment, discrimination, and limited access to community and societal resources. Stated positively, a social justice prevention perspective promotes social change that works to reduce discriminatory forces within society with the goals of empowering people and providing greater access to societal institutions, such as those that provide quality health care, education, and employment opportunities.

Prilleltensky (2012) has written an excellent conceptualization and application of the relationship between justice and wellness (or well-being), arguing that experiences of injustice at societal, organizational (i.e., work), interpersonal, and intrapersonal levels can lead to major problems at all levels. The four levels of well-being are measured by six objective and subjective domains of wellness or indicators. For example, one economic objective indicator of intrapersonal well-being is money for medical care, and a subjective indicator is feeling secure financially. At the societal level of well-being, an objective indicator of well-being might be employment opportunities, and at the subjective level are indicators such as personal safety and equality. Prilleltensky discusses subtypes of justice—societal (community), interpersonal, intrapersonal, and organizational—and presents an ecological model showing the interrelationship between justice and well-being, explicitly making the connection between fairness and well-being. This framework specifically demonstrates the importance of social justice and fairness and their relationship to overall well-being at multiple levels, from wellness at the individual level to broader societal levels.

Within a prevention framework, social justice interventions may take the form of advocating for laws and public policy decisions that promote the health and welfare of all citizens of a community, state, or nation. Specific examples might include social advocacy for sufficient educational funding and student integration across the educational landscape so that all students in a school district and community have equal access to quality education. On a local school level, prevention in an individual school building might include promoting school programs and activities so that all students have equal access and opportunities to participate. A prevention specialist might also work with school staff so that their school-based concerns can be addressed from a prevention orientation rather than waiting until issues reach crisis levels, for example, bullying prevention. At a curricular level, school counselors might intervene with a school curriculum committee to address concerns that students present about a particular subject or instructor. This might result in better placement of students in the course, adjustments in pedagogy, or extra course assistance for students. This type of intervention, requiring dialogue with those teaching the course, is likely to result in a better outcome for students as well as instructors.

Morsillo and Prilleltensky (2007) describe innovative social action programs that were developed by disempowered youth in two Australian communities. Two interventions were guided by the concept of psychopolitical validity (Prilleltensky, 2003). Psychopolitical validity "refers to the extent to which research and action take into account power dynamics in psychological and political domains affecting oppression, liberation, and wellness at the personal, group, and community levels" (Morsillo & Prilleltensky, 2007, p. 726).

Youth in one intervention group were a diverse group of high school students from a very low-income community in the Australian state of Victoria. School disengagement and retention were common problems among students in this community; students were encouraged to participate in the intervention by teachers who identified them as at-risk for becoming more disengaged from school. The main objectives of the intervention were to increase personal sociopolitical awareness, to develop group organizational skills, and to develop community problem-solving skills. Through the intervention, students were encouraged to think critically about their own concerns with the community, how they might identify needed corrections in the community, and actions that they may take to improve the community. The intervention included student-initiated drug-free dance parties, a theater company for student performances, and developing activities for children at a refugee cultural festival. The intervention was evaluated through qualitative assessments. The assessments yielded positive results for individuals, the student group as a whole, and the community. Outcomes reported for individual students included enhanced sociopolitical awareness and increased social responsibility and hopefulness. At a group level, the groups operated effectively, and they developed cohesiveness and solidarity. The community benefited from increased positive youth involvement in the community. All but one of the five community projects were successfully completed through this intervention.

The second intervention was a social group of same-sex attracted adolescents and young adults, aged 16 to 21 years. The group consisted of 16 members from different ethnic groups, evenly divided among males and females. Eleven of the members were in high school or college, and others were either employed or unemployed and homeless. This intervention had similar objectives as the previous intervention. Members of the group were aware of homophobic attitudes in the community and discrimination.

Therefore, their community project focused on developing a drama production that addressed homophobia. The outcomes of this intervention suggested that the participants valued the opportunity for self-expression, and the performance promoted assertiveness. Peer acceptance and support were generated at the group level. The community benefited through increased awareness about homophobia and oppression that homophobia fosters. Similar to the first intervention with high school students, the community benefited through positive youth involvement in the community as a result of this second intervention.

Interventions such as those described above have the potential to yield multiple benefits at the individual, group, and community levels. They can help individuals develop personal skills that empower them and enhance their development. The interventions also teach individuals about the power of working within the context of small groups, and they also can be transformative for the communities in which they are carried out.

As in the examples above, a social justice perspective applied to prevention will seek to prevent individual problems and promote health-enhancing behaviors and opportunities through systemic interventions at local levels (e.g., schools, neighborhoods) or more broadly (e.g., state and federal legislation). Kenny, Horne, Orpinas, and Reese (2009) edited an excellent volume that gives examples of social justice perspectives in different contexts, including schools and workplaces. The volume also describes a vision for promoting a social justice prevention agenda for the future, including the elimination of social barriers that prevent people from maximizing health outcomes. A vision of social justice has much to offer as a framework for prevention and health promotion in the 21st century.

Activity

Describe two or three major problems in your community that would benefit from a social justice prevention intervention. How might you address these problems through social action or advocacy?

3

Guidelines for Prevention Practice, Research, and Education

I n addition to theoretical approaches, scholars have outlined best practices in prevention (Hage et al., 2007). This set of 15 Guidelines first published by Hage et al. (2007) has since evolved, under the leadership of a Work Group of psychologists, into a set of 9 Prevention Guidelines, summarized in Table 3.1. The Guidelines have been discussed and reviewed by psychologists, through meetings and conferences and through a period of public review and comment. The Guidelines have also been reviewed by the American Psychological Association (APA) boards, committees, and divisions. Throughout the review process, the Guidelines have been revised to address comments of stakeholders. The initial goal is for the Guidelines to be approved by APA Council as recommendations to psychologists and then eventually disseminated widely for use by psychologists and other prevention specialists. At the time of this writing, the Guidelines are under review by APA and, therefore, are considered to be in draft form.

The Prevention Guidelines address important areas of prevention work of psychologists and other prevention specialists, and the discussion of them in this book of Best Practices is important. The Guidelines are also designed to encourage psychologists, counselors, and other prevention specialists to develop their knowledge, skills, and training competencies in prevention practice, research, and public policy making.

A review of the Guidelines shows that best practices in prevention are recommended in several areas. First, prevention interventions are best if they are based on evidence-based and theory-driven practices (Guideline 1). Too often, prevention interventions are offered with little empirical evidence to support their use and with weak theoretical foundations. Fortunately, in recent years, prevention practitioners have access to national registries that list empirically supported prevention interventions (e.g., National Registry of Evidence-Based Programs and Practices [NREPP] supported by the U.S. Department of Health and Human Services, Substance Abuse and Mental Health Services Administration [www.nrepp.samhsa.gov]). Second, it is critically important that prevention specialists use culturally appropriate

Table 3.1   Summary: Guidelines for Prevention Practice, Research, and Education

Guideline 1: Psychologists are encouraged to select and implement preventive interventions that are theory and evidence based.
Guideline 2: Psychologists are encouraged to use culturally relevant prevention practices adapted to the specific context in which they are implemented.
Guideline 3: Psychologists are encouraged to develop and implement interventions that reduce risks and promote human strengths.
Guideline 4: Psychologists are encouraged to incorporate research and evaluation as an integral part of preventive program development and implementation, including consideration of environmental contexts that impact prevention.
Guideline 5: Psychologists are encouraged to consider ethical issues in prevention research and practice.
Guideline 6: Psychologists are encouraged to attend to contextual issues of social disparity that may inform prevention practice and research.
Guideline 7: Psychologists are encouraged to increase their awareness, knowledge, and skills essential to prevention through continuing education, training, supervision, and consultation.
Guideline 8: Psychologists are encouraged to engage in systemic and institutional interventions that strengthen the health of individuals, families, and communities and prevent psychological and physical distress and disability.
Guideline 9: Psychologists are encouraged to inform the deliberation of public policies that promote health and well-being when relevant prevention science findings are available.

Note: As of this writing (June 2012), the Guidelines are in draft form until approved by APA Council. A complete document may be requested from the authors of this book.

prevention interventions (Guideline 2). Prevention specialists are encouraged to consult with relevant groups and stakeholders from the very beginning of developing a prevention intervention and to maintain contact and consultation throughout the process. It is highly recommended that individuals and groups affected by a prevention intervention be consulted about the problem to be addressed. It is also recommended that stakeholders reach consensus about (a) the most effective way or ways to intervene and deliver the intervention, (b) how best to collect process and outcome data to evaluate the intervention, (c) potential ethical issues, and (d) strategies to disseminate results of the intervention to stakeholders and the larger community. This can be a lengthy process and requires prevention specialists to develop rapport with stakeholders and sustain a relationship with them throughout the process, from planning through dissemination and beyond. A long-term commitment of community collaboration is important to help ensure the sustainability of prevention activities beyond the initial intervention. A strong community collaborative process will help ensure that prevention interventions are culturally appropriate and relevant to the communities involved, whether they are neighborhoods, schools, or work places.

In addition to preventing problem behaviors, it is imperative that prevention specialists be mindful of interventions that reduce risks and promote strengths and protective factors of the population or community being served (Guideline 3). This type of activity can take different forms. For example, children and adolescents can be assisted in identifying interpersonal and emotional strengths and how best to utilize them in making healthy and sound decisions about their behaviors. Perspectives from positive psychology will be useful in this activity. Measures to identify individual strengths are available commercially and could be used to increase the self-awareness (e.g., *StrengthsFinder* [www.strengthsfinder.com]; DAP [Search Institute]). As another example, health promotion in the work place may include advocating for healthy food choices in company cafeterias and seminars on strategies to manage work-related stress. Attention to protective characteristics and health-enhancing behaviors will increase awareness of protective factors and reduce risks for problem behaviors.

Guideline 4 recommends that psychologists and other prevention specialists engage in evaluation and research processes to assess the efficacy and effectiveness of their interventions. It is recommended that prevention interventions be initiated after consideration of their appropriateness for the community or population groups that will be the recipients of the intervention. This can be accomplished in different ways, such as through literature reviews of empirical evidence supporting an intervention for use with the targeted population, focus groups of stakeholders, and recipients of the interventions, by conducting a pilot study of the intervention, and by using elicitation research to identify variables most salient to participants to better inform the prevention intervention (see TRA/PB in Chapter 2). Examples of elicitation research can be found in Fishbein and Ajzen (2010) and Romano and Netland (2008).

Guideline 5 encourages prevention specialists to give strong consideration to ethical issues when engaging in prevention research and practice. In terms of ethics, there are unique considerations that are not addressed in the traditional ethical codes of the professions. For example, when a universal or primary prevention intervention is delivered to an entire school or community, prevention specialists do not require informed consent and participants are not asked to volunteer for the intervention. Primary prevention interventions are assumed to be good for everyone, and they usually are, for example, programs that encourage children and parents to substitute sedentary leisure activity with alternatives that encourage physical activity to improve physical, emotional, and relational health. However, in some cases, it may be difficult for families to implement such a recommendation without guidance on ways to reduce impediments such as those related to time and resources and physical abilities. When designing secondary, selective, or indicated prevention interventions, it is important that the at-risk groups are not stigmatized by the intervention, for example, developing alcohol and drug prevention programs only in low social-economic communities.

Guideline 6 addresses issues of social disparities across the society and recommends that they be given strong consideration in prevention research and practice. The late George Albee, past president of the APA, strongly advocated for many years, until his death in 2006, for a social justice prevention perspective. It is recommended that prevention specialists consider negative social conditions, such as poverty, oppression, and discrimination in their prevention research and applications, and develop interventions to reduce such conditions. Negative social conditions contribute to individual and community problems and lead people to feel disempowered and discriminated against. These negative social conditions contribute to major societal problems such as disparities in health care, educational outcomes, career opportunities, and income levels of disenfranchised members of the community and larger society.

Guideline 7 encourages psychologists and prevention specialists to strengthen their training in prevention. It is recommended that faculty who develop formal degree training curricula in colleges and universities include prevention content as part of the training either through stand-alone courses or the infusion of prevention content across the curriculum (Conyne, Newmeyer, Kenny, Romano, & Matthews, 2008). This Guideline also encourages more informal continuing education of practicing psychologists and other prevention specialists through individual study, attendance at conferences, and collaboration with more experienced prevention professionals.

Guidelines 8 and 9, while related, are different, and thus, their separation is merited. Guideline 8 recommends that prevention specialists engage in research and practices that strengthen institutions such as schools, families, and workplaces to help them become more health enhancing for people who learn, live, and work in them. It encourages prevention activities at the systemic level to promote environments that enhance health and well-being. Guideline 9 is broader and encourages prevention specialists to influence public policy by informing and educating policy makers and major stakeholders with relevant prevention science information during their deliberations about policies and laws important to health and well-being. Examples of public policy initiatives that may be informed by prevention science include policies to remove barriers to quality educational opportunities and quality health services to segments of the population, laws that more strongly enforce illegal sales of tobacco and alcohol to minors, and laws that protect human rights.

Activity

Table 3.1 lists Nine Best Practice Guidelines for Prevention. As you review these guidelines, how might they be implemented with your current or future prevention activities?

4

Research-Informed Prevention Practice

Learning From the Wisdom of Science

We can't solve problems by using the same kind of thinking we used when we created them.

—Albert Einstein

As we continue to discuss steps to be considered by prevention practitioners as they engage with others in developing and delivering prevention projects, we turn to the topic of how research informs prevention practice. The integration of scientific findings into practice has long been considered a goal of the behavioral sciences (Albee, 1987; Wandersman et al., 1998). However, in recent years, this goal has become more a reality, as prevention practice is increasingly guided by science and the dissemination of research findings has become a major focus in policy and project implementation. One place to begin the process of informing prevention practice is with an understanding of evidence-based interventions.

Empirically Supported Prevention Applications

It is highly recommended that the prevention specialist investigate the appropriateness of a prevention intervention for a particular group or environmental context, as well as identify and select interventions that have been supported empirically. There are different resources that the prevention specialist can access for appropriate programs, but one of the most comprehensive resources has been developed by the Substance Abuse and Mental Services Administration (SAMHSA; www.samhsa.gov). SAMHSA is a government entity within the U.S. Department of Health and Human Services that works to prevent alcohol and drug abuse and to improve mental health services. SAMHSA publishes NREPP (www.nrepp.samhsa.gov). While NREPP is not an exhaustive list of prevention programs, the Registry lists programs that have been reviewed and shown to be empirically supported.

The Registry is available online and is easy to use to search for specific types of prevention programs of interest to the prevention specialist. For example, the prevention specialist may be interested in alcohol prevention programs for middle school students, and this topic and population group can be searched for on the NREPP website. NREPP also lists research that supports the specific intervention, rates the quality of the research, and describes the strengths and limitations of the research. An interested user of the intervention can readily review the research and, perhaps, contact authors for additional consultation about the intervention. NREPP also provides other information about the intervention, such as whether it is designed as a universal, selective, or indicated prevention intervention, and the cost of the intervention. Readers searching for a research-supported prevention intervention are encouraged to consult NREPP as an initial step to determine if one of the programs listed on the Registry is appropriate for their application.

Another U.S. government agency, the Office of Juvenile Justice and Delinquency Prevention (OJJDP; www.ojjdp.gov) is an excellent online resource to locate model prevention programs that are evidenced based and, especially, those that may be useful in preventing youth bullying, aggressive behaviors, and criminal activity. More than 200 programs are reviewed on the OJJDP website. Similar to NREPP, the OJJDP resource is easy to use and allows the user to narrow the search to characteristics most germane for specific objectives and population groups.

One nongovernment organization, the Coalition of Evidence-Based Policy (http://evidencebasedprograms.org/wordpress), is a nonprofit, nonpartisan organization that seeks to strengthen government and public policies and interventions designed to promote improved social policies, such as those related to educational reform, reduction of poverty, and crime prevention. The Coalition reviews and evaluates the most promising social interventions that are supported by empirical research. Working with the U.S. federal government, the Coalition has helped shape U.S. national policies on several social initiatives, including those to prevent teen pregnancy, to improve education and employment outcomes for workers, and to strengthen investments in low-income communities. It is recommended that prevention specialists interested in social policies and social reform review the Coalition's website for information and reviews about promising social interventions that support prevention goals.

These are only a few of the organizations and agencies that can be helpful in identifying empirically supported prevention interventions. It is recommended that prevention specialists be mindful of the importance of selecting prevention interventions that not only meet the needs of the group or institution targeted for the prevention intervention but also attempt, as much as possible, to select interventions that have been supported empirically. As one can see by perusing the large number of interventions reviewed by the agencies and organizations cited above, there are likely to be several intervention options to meet prevention objectives. Since the interventions reviewed have been empirically supported, the websites are excellent resources to start the search for an appropriate prevention application.

The prevention specialist may prefer to either develop his or her own intervention or search the literature for interventions that are not listed on one of the agency or organization websites. The intervention desired or the population to be served may be so specialized that the prevention specialist prefers to develop his or her own. However, in this situation, it is extremely important that the intervention be developed in consultation with major stakeholders of the intervention. Stakeholders might be community leaders, leaders of the setting where the intervention will be delivered, and groups targeted to receive the intervention. Principles of informed consent will also require that the prevention specialist identify the intervention as experimental or as a pilot program, if no or little empirical data supports its use. Elicitation research, as discussed in Chapter 2 with the Theory of Reasoned Action and Planned Behavior, is one methodology that can help inform the prevention specialist about the most salient variables to bring about change with the population that will eventually receive the prevention intervention. Other methodologies can also be helpful in development of a new prevention intervention, such as conducting needs assessments and focus groups of major stakeholders of the proposed prevention intervention.

As noted above, efforts to identify empirically supported prevention interventions have expanded, as has their dissemination by scientific and governmental organizations (e.g., Bumgarger & Perkins, 2009; President's New Freedom Commission on Mental Health, 2003; U.S. Public Health Service, Office of the Surgeon General, 2004). Several factors appear to support this expansion of the integration of scientific findings into practice. One factor is recent efforts to move toward the development of a registry of preventive trials. While several informative topic-specific compilations of effective research exist (e.g., NREPP), which will be discussed in detail below, no one broad-based registry of preventive intervention trials yet exists; however, several scholars have initiated such efforts. For example, Dr. C. Hendricks Brown, with the support of the Society for Prevention Research (SPR), is constructing a registry called the International Registry of Preventive Trials, which would cover the prevention of substance abuse, delinquency and crime, mental health problems, suicide, child maltreatment, and HIV/AIDS and other sexually transmitted diseases. The registry will provide researchers, policy makers, and practitioners with scientific information about an intervention's success, based on the quality of its design and strength of research findings, and include information about the cost, availability of training, and implementation (Brown, 2011).

Second, a registry of preventive trials is now possible because scientists are closer to reaching consensus about the standards for identifying interventions for dissemination. For example, in 2004, SPR, led by a committee of prevention scientists, unanimously approved a set of Standards of Evidence, which identify and list programs and policies that have been tested and shown to be efficacious or effective. These standards were published in a journal article, written collectively by SPR's committee on standards of evidence chaired by Brian Flay (Flay et al., 2005).

The SPR standards address three levels in the identification of preventive interventions. These levels are efficacious, effective, and ready for dissemination. A prevention intervention is considered "efficacious" when it has been tested in at least two rigorous trials that involve (a) defined samples from defined populations, (b) psychometrically sound measures and data collection, (c) rigorous statistical approaches, (d) consistent positive effects, and (e) significant findings maintained through at least one long-term follow-up. An "effective" intervention will not only meet all standards for efficacious interventions but will also (a) offer manuals, training, and technical support to support implementation; (b) be evaluated under real-world conditions; (c) demonstrate the practical importance of intervention outcome effects; and (d) specify the population to whom findings can be generalized. Finally, preventive interventions considered "ready for dissemination" will not only meet all standards for efficacious and effective interventions but will also provide (a) evidence of an ability to "go to scale", (b) cost information, and (c) monitoring and evaluation tools (Flay et al., 2005, p. 169).

Finally, scientifically informed practice has recently advanced because the numbers of empirically supported mental health, drug abuse prevention, and health promotion programs have grown significantly in recent years. Several scholars have presented aggregate evidence across multiple studies to successfully demonstrate the efficacy of prevention interventions in diverse settings and populations (Catalano, Berglund, Ryan, Lonczak, & Hawkins, 2002; Greenberg, Domitrovich, & Bumbarger, 2001; O'Connell, Boat, & Warner, 2009; Weisz, Sandler, Durlak, & Anton, 2005). For example, Weisz et al. (2005) details the efforts of several work groups who have identified more than 125 empirically supported prevention programs to illustrate different forms of effective preventive interventions. These programs include health promotion and positive youth development programs, universal (or primary) prevention programs with children, selective (secondary) prevention programs with adults and families, and indicated (tertiary) prevention programs with youth. A review of the specific characteristics of these evidence-based approaches increases our understanding of what works in prevention practice.

_____ Components of Successful Prevention Programs

A number of components of successful prevention programs can be gleaned from the literature describing effective interventions. Enhanced awareness of these components may help practitioners effectively select and create more effective programs. What we have learned from studies of successful preventive interventions is that they are typically theory driven, comprehensive (multicomponent interventions and of sufficient dosage), and socially and culturally relevant; have a strong generative base, addressing multiple ecological levels (e.g., individual, family, school, community); are aimed at both person- and environment-centered change; are developmentally appropriate; are led by an interdisciplinary team; use varied teaching methods (usually active and skills based); and are delivered across multiple contexts or settings (Nation et al., 2003; Walsh, DePaul, & Park-Taylor, 2009).

In addition, effective programs have well-trained staff and often support positive relationships with adults and peers (Durlak, 2003, Nation et al., 2003; Rotheram-Borus & Duan, 2003). Effective dissemination of prevention research is necessary to inform the public, government officials, and other professionals about effective practices and to create systemic change (Kenny & Hage, 2009; Rotheram-Borus & Duan, 2003). Furthermore, additional research is needed to better understand the effects of developing or adapting prevention and treatment programs for specific cultural and language groups (Weisz et al., 2005).

An example of a program with these components is the Asian/Pacific Islander Youth Violence Prevention Center (APIYVPC) at the University of Hawaii. The APIYVPC Program is a comprehensive violence prevention research project that aims to reduce and prevent interpersonal youth violence among the Asian and Pacific Islander (API) population by collaborating with the community to conduct rigorous and culturally responsive research, as well as to create a national prototype for public health in the API community (Guerrero, Goebert, Alicata, & Bell, 2009; Umemoto et al., 2009). The leadership team of APIYVPC includes a Community Advisory Board, Scientific Advisory Board, Executive Committee, Senior Scientists/Mentors, and community workgroups with professionals from a variety of backgrounds, such as psychology, social work, psychiatry, public health, urban and regional planning, and sociology (Umemoto et al., 2009).

APIYVPC incorporates the community by partnering with local organizations and schools to address community needs by, for example, the creation of a local high school student task force, a women's support group for mothers recovering from substance abuse, and a teacher and counselor workgroup (Umemoto et al., 2009). APIYVPC efforts have included disseminating research about violence prevention for a specific population that has been previously overlooked and not studied, as well as conducting community focus groups for a needs assessment for youth prevention and intervention programs. APIYVPC has also conducted research on prevalence and on risk and protective factors related to youth violence in Hawaii (Guerrero et al., 2009; Umemoto et al., 2009). As stated in the program's mission, APIYVPC aims to create a national prototype by developing an effective, comprehensive, public health and culturally competent model for the API community (APIYVPC, 2010).

In addition to disseminating their research through scholarly publications and local student presentations, the program also trains local community leaders in conducting methodologically sound research and program evaluation and in how to analyze and present scientific data (APIYVPC, 2010). In addition, APIYVPC regularly conducts training seminars on various topics (e.g., grant writing to facilitate career development for student researchers and API staff). The APIYVPC's promotion of prevention research and evaluation, as well as collaboration at multiple ecological levels has established a comprehensive and sustainable program. Through constant evaluation, APIYVPC allows for flexibility and innovation, which works to facilitate a community-wide reduction in youth violence (Umemoto et al., 2009). More information on the APIYVPC can be found at http://apiyvpc.org/.

Targeting Risk and Protective Factors

Many professionals who specialize in the design and implementation of preventive interventions stress the importance of designing preventive interventions that target both risk and protective factors in individuals, families, and communities (Kenny et al., 2009; Kumper & Summerhays, 2006). Protective and risk factors occur both on an individual and societal level, thus, affecting people within multiple communities and systems. Also, with few exceptions, risk and protective factors are not simply opposites along a continuum of risk and protection. For example, poverty is a risk factor but wealth is not a protective factor (Durlak, 1998). Hence, risk and protection need to be considered and assessed separately when engaging in prevention practice and research. Finally, risk and/or protective factors may operate differentially for particular social and cultural groups, and important within-group differences may exist. Hence, practitioners need to consider how individuals and groups within a cultural community may be differentially affected by factors such as socioeconomic status, geography, acculturation/enculturation, and immigration status (Reese & Vera, 2007).

Risk Factors

Hence, to begin, prevention practitioners may choose to focus their programs on reducing or eliminating a set of identified risk factors. Some risk factors that have been identified in the literature as important to consider in designing effective prevention programs include living in an impoverished neighborhood, poor quality schools, peer rejection, parental psychopathology, early onset of a problem, and punitive child rearing (Durlak, 1998). Evidence also points to the accumulation of multiple risks as most significant in leading to poor outcomes for individuals and families. For example, while little difference in adjustment appears to exist between children exposed to one out of six risk factors compared with those exposed to none, children exposed to four or more risk factors were shown to experience 20 times, rather than 4 to 6 times, the rate of psychological problems as children exposed to one or no risk factors (Rutter, 1979).

An example of how a risk factor can be incorporated into or addressed within a prevention emphasis is found in the Adolescent Transitions Program (ATP). The ATP is a multilevel, family-centered, school-based intervention targeting youth who are at risk for problem behavior or substance use. The focus of the intervention targets the specific risk factor of coercive parenting strategies in the development of problem behaviors in youth. Parents are taught active parenting skills such as making requests, using rewards, monitoring, making rules, providing reasonable consequences for rule violations, problem solving, and active listening. The curriculum for teens teaches how to set realistic goals for behavior change and how to define reasonable steps toward these goals, developing peer support for prosocial and abstinent behavior, setting limits, and problem solving. Results from two separate randomized clinical trials revealed significant improvements in family interactions and positive parenting practices. In addition, teens' externalizing and antisocial behaviors were significantly reduced after their parents participated in ATP (Connell, Dishion, Yasui, & Kavanagh, 2007).

Protective Factors

Protective factors may be described as the ability or potential that at-risk individuals and communities have to develop strengths, despite negative environmental circumstances that might put them at greater risk of negative outcomes (e.g., poverty, prejudice, discrimination) (Walsh et al., 2009). Examples of protective factors include positive relationships, self-efficacy, community involvement, and academic achievement. In addition, while these factors do not prevent at-risk individuals and communities from facing social injustice, they do increase the likelihood of positive outcomes for those who face challenges or obstacles related to their community, school, or home environment. Furthermore, at the environmental level, a number of systems and policy approaches have been identified as having an enduring impact on resilience and improving child outcomes. These approaches include child- and family-friendly policy interventions, such as the availability of high quality child care, early preschool education, and family support programs, as well as media campaigns, political advocacy, and community efforts to organize or affiliate with grassroots organizations to address social problems, like racism and poverty (Vera, Buhin, & Isacco, 2009).

A final point that prevention practitioners need to consider relative to their decision about what type of intervention to choose when working to reduce or eliminate risk factors and enhance protective factors is the level of the intervention. For example, if a practitioner decides to focus his or her program on strengthening the protective factor of parental engagement, the choice about how to design the intervention to help families and parents be better parents will depend on whether one wishes to focus on primary prevention (before the problem begins), secondary prevention (reduces or eliminates risk factors or targets those at early stages of the problem), or tertiary prevention (reduces debilitating effects of an existing problem). A program for primary prevention might target new parents and their infants in a child care center to enhance knowledge of effective parenting practices, while an intervention focused on secondary prevention might target parents of teens who are experiencing academic difficulty, and finally, an intervention focused on tertiary prevention might target parents of teens who have committed a crime.

Translating Research to Practice

As we conclude this chapter of the book, which provides important foundational knowledge and recommendations from the scientific community for prevention practitioners in preparing to engage in prevention practice and research, we highlight some of the key findings that have been described thus far. To begin, practitioners engaging in prevention are encouraged to develop programs from a sound theoretical base, as such programs have been shown to be most effective. In addition, ensuring that resources are put to best use requires that prevention practitioners engage in rigorous program evaluation, targeting the specific goals and cultural contexts of the prevention program.

Hence, it is essential that prevention programs be designed, selected, and implemented with a specific cultural context in mind and with the involvement and input of members of the target community. Such programs are more likely to be sustained and to be relevant to the lives of the participants. Finally, prevention practitioners are encouraged to focus their efforts not only on reducing risks, such as school failure or family dysfunction, but also to simultaneously work to build strengths and protective factors, such as social and communication skills and career readiness. Prevention practice that combines the reduction of risk with the promotion of strengths is more apt to empower participants to successfully gain control of their life course.

In the next chapter, key elements in the practice of prevention will be highlighted, including the use of empirically supported prevention applications, the essential aspects of collaboration, social and cultural relevance, ethical issues in prevention practice, and the importance of program dissemination.

Activity

Review at least two of the websites identified in this chapter, and in each, search for two prevention interventions that might meet the needs of your organization or population. Critique the programs you selected as to their applicability for your setting.

5

Social Justice and Prevention

We have no choice really. To be neutral in a situation of injustice is to have chosen sides already.

—Desmond Tutu (Tutu & Tutu, 2007, p. 8)

According to Prilleltensky and Nelson (2009), 99% of prevention interventions that are currently being implemented are individually focused, as opposed to systems focused, that is, focused on changing organizations, institutions, and structures that may contribute to or serve as obstacles to changing oppressive circumstances. Prevention specialists need to thoughtfully discern when an individually based change or intervention is needed versus one that is aimed at a change in the social context, social milieu, or social system. Hence, prevention practitioners need knowledge, skills, and increased awareness to recognize how problems are environmentally based.

Preventive interventions that promote social justice are often designed as systemic interventions that reduce inequality in a variety of settings such as schools and communities (Kenny et al., 2009). These prevention programs work to simultaneously increase competencies and decrease problems in people in order to empower them in three ways: (1) by giving them knowledge they need to more effectively deal with situations of unequal social power, (2) by teaching them skills that can be used to address such situations in a healthy manner, and (3) by changing social policies that may serve as barriers in the promotion of social justice. Successful interventions provide youth, families, and communities with the tools and motivation needed to create change on a systemic level and promote social justice (Conyne, 2010). As stated by Albee (1982), "We must recognize the fact that no mass disorder affecting large numbers of human beings has ever been controlled or eliminated by attempts at treating each affected individual or by training enough professionals as interventionists" (p. 1045).

Furthermore, the process of engaging in social change and advocacy has a long-standing tradition in fields such as psychology, social work, and public health (Kiselica & Robinson, 2001; Toporek, Lewis, & Crethar, 2009).

Indeed, the roots of the social advocacy and social justice movement can be traced to the very beginnings of the helping fields (Hartung & Blustein, 2002). More recently, scholars across several specialty areas have urged professional helpers from psychology and related helping fields to broaden their roles and responsibilities to incorporate social advocacy and a critical consciousness of power and privilege among historically oppressed groups both inside and outside the therapeutic context (Bemak, 2005; Hage & Kenny, 2009; Toporek, Gerstein, Fouad, Roysircar, & Israel, 2006; Vera & Speight, 2007).

Hence, you might ask, to what extent is social justice work necessary in doing prevention? Our response is that social justice is absolutely essential to engaging in the work of prevention. Recognizing oppression is no longer enough; prevention specialists, researchers, and educators must go beyond traditional roles to act in order to remove complex social, political, and economic barriers faced by individuals and communities who are marginalized. Efforts to promote social justice are integral to active efforts to promote the collective health and well-being of individuals and communities and, thus, is a predominant value *underlying* the work of prevention (Prilleltensky & Nelson, 2009). Indeed, it has been suggested that the ethical practice of prevention needs to include efforts aimed at social change and the elimination of injustice (Hage & Kenny, 2009).

Social justice and prevention can be viewed as symbiotic, and the majority of prevention work has systemic and societal implications (Kenny & Hage, 2009; Price & Behrens, 2003; Vera & Speight, 2007). Prevention practitioners have the responsibility to address societal issues of oppression and exploitation (Perry & Albee, 1994; Schwartz & Lindley, 2009). Therefore, in doing prevention work, prevention practitioners must understand and deal ethically with the complex interchange of social forces, such as racism and poverty, in creating and sustaining socially just prevention interventions. They have an ethical responsibility to strive to be agents of social justice in the communities in which they work (Hage, 2005; Vera & Speight, 2007).

Social and Cultural Relevance in Prevention

Prevention-oriented professionals have become increasingly aware that contextual variables like class, gender, race, disability, and sexual orientation unavoidably affect the mental health and well-being of individuals and communities (Albee, 2000; Kenny & Hage, 2009).

In addition, a unique ethical challenge to prevention work is the necessity of respecting the social and cultural differences of prevention program participants and communities (Reese & Vera, 2007). Although the danger of value imposition and ethnocentric interventions also exists in individual therapy (Sue & Sue, 2008), the risks of inappropriately imposing one's values are perhaps even greater for prevention interventions, since they often involve multiple ecological levels and no single identified "client," which complicates the process of obtaining adequate informed consent. In addition, each stage of prevention intervention (development, implementation, evaluation) involves value-laden decisions (Danish, 1990).

Therefore, it is imperative that prevention specialists understand the impact of their own culture and become aware of the values and biases that underlie their prevention work (Sanson-Fisher & Turnbull, 1987). It is also important that professionals communicate these values clearly to the target population (Watts, 1994). If cultural values and biases are not adequately addressed in prevention efforts, there is a danger that prevention practitioners will impose their values in an oppressive way that may be damaging to the target population (Trickett, 1998; Trickett & Levin, 1990).

The work of Reese and Vera (2007) supports the importance of examining values and beliefs held by prevention specialists in making prevention work culturally relevant. Cultural relevance is defined as matching values and beliefs between the intervention and the community it intends to serve (Reese & Vera, 2007). Cultural relevance can have an impact on participant participation, satisfaction, retention, and acceptance of the program (Reese & Vera, 2007). The importance of making sure prevention efforts are culturally relevant is consistent with the recognition that primary prevention is an act of "premeditated intrusion into the lives and settings of individuals and groups" (Trickett & Levin, 1990, p. 9).

Black Parenting Strengths and Strategies Program

An illustration of a prevention program that incorporates attention to cultural relevance is The Black Parenting Strengths and Strategies program (BPSS). The BPSS is an intervention program for low-income African American families that targets parenting practices associated with early development of conduct problems in children (Coard, Foy-Watson, Zimmer, & Wallace, 2007). Families in BPSS meet weekly in 2-hour sessions for 12 weeks (Coard et al., 2007). The theoretical foundation of the program is Ogbu's (1981) cultural–ecological model and Ward's (2000) theory on the impact of culture on parenting behavior. Ward (2000) states that it is African American parents' role to protect their children and teach them how to cope with hostility, prejudice, and discrimination they may experience from the dominant culture.

BPSS uses the well-established, empirically supported Parenting the Strong-Willed Child program (PSWC; Forehand & Long, 2002) and actively promotes positive racial socialization, defined as "the process by which messages are transmitted or communicated inter- and intra-generationally regarding the significance and meaning of race and ethnicity" (Coard et al., 2007, p. 801). Results from program evaluations indicate that PSWC improves the parent–child relationship and increases positive child behaviors by teaching parents universally adaptive child noncompliance management and prevention skills (Coard et al., 2007). BPSS utilizes the skills taught in

PSWC, such as attending, rewarding, ignoring, giving effective directions, and using time-outs appropriately to prevent behavior problems (Coard et al., 2007). By integrating PSWC with strategies promoting positive racial socialization, BPSS is better able to serve the target population.

In the development of BPSS, intentional efforts were made to ensure that the content and delivery reflected the values and traditions of the African American family participants (Coard et al., 2007). For example, the African American perspective use of *we* and African proverbs, poems, symbols, and prayers were incorporated into the content of the program. Also, content addressing the challenges of advocating for one's child on issues of curriculum bias or low teacher expectations and dealing with overt and subtle incidences of racism, prejudice, and discrimination was integrated into the program (Coard et al., 2007). In addition, BPSS builds on strengths of African American families and teaches parenting skills within a sociocultural and sociopolitical context (Coard et al., 2007). For example, session topics include the social and emotional development in Black children, increasing children's confidence in school environments, developing positive self-image in Black children, promoting positive and developmentally appropriate parent–child discussions about racial issues, and enhancing children's problem-solving skills (Coard et al., 2007). BPSS is an exceptional example of how prevention practitioners can blend an evidence-based approach with culturally relevant strategies to implement an effective prevention program. To find out more information about BPSS, visit http://sites.google.com/site/uncgaafss/home.

Importance of Collaboration and Community Involvement

Community-based collaboration involves the pooling of resources, power, and authority among groups within a community to bring about mutually beneficial goals (Bond & Carmola Hauf, 2007; Davidson & Bowen, 2011). The benefits, strengths, and challenges of such collaboration often between academic and community partners in conducting prevention research and practice are many. Both gain new perspectives and understanding, and additional resources are often made available to community groups. Ideally, the partnership constitutes a best practice critical for achieving effective prevention (Bond & Carmola Hauf, 2007) and forms bridges between academicians and community agencies that can improve services offered to individuals, while also providing rich sources of data (Davidson & Bowen, 2011).

Yet the history of this partnership is sometimes tainted by negative experiences community practitioners have had with researchers, including a "drive-by research" approach, and interpretation of findings in ways that reflect negatively on community members or fall short of understanding how to appropriately translate findings into recommendations for practice (Jordan, 2011). Critical dialogue and intentional efforts toward understanding are needed to develop a truly collaborative model of engaging in community-based research. In all prevention work, dynamics of privilege and power exist between prevention specialists and community members; prevention research needs to involve the community in determining the research goals and methods so as to ensure that programs are developed to meet the community's specific needs.

Creating successful community collaborations necessitates new roles for prevention practitioners and raises unique ethical concerns. Ethical issues are created in the effort to establish a true partnership that takes account of power dynamics and privilege. In addition, academic partners need to take care to maintain confidentiality with multiple partners as the intervention is conducted. Models such as participatory action research (PAR; Kidd & Kral, 2005) and community-based participatory research (Israel, Schultz, Parker, & Becker, 1998) provide a structure and guidance to empower community partners in the effort to create true community collaboration. PAR involves all relevant partners in actively examining and reflecting on the historical, political, cultural, economic, and geographic contexts. PAR strives to be active with co-research, conducted by and for those to be helped. In this process, those to be helped determine the purposes and outcomes of their own inquiry (Wadsworth, 1998).

Hence, essential to developing a collaborative relationship in prevention efforts is the need for practitioners and researchers to demonstrate trustworthiness, respect, and sensitivity to the perspectives of community partners as well as participants (Davidson & Bowen, 2011). The cultures of the communities affected by a preventive intervention vary enormously; prevention specialists must understand their cultural values and biases and avoid imposing them on the targeted population. Recommendations to assist this process include (a) developing positive working relationships with community members and (b) developing and implementing programs that are valued by the community (Reese & Vera, 2007).

Reaching Out About Depression

An example of a program that uses community collaboration to empower participants is housed in the Cambridge Health Alliance's Department of Community Affairs. Women of low socioeconomic status tend to experience higher rates of interpersonal partner violence and sexual assault, as well as stressful life conditions, more physical health problems, higher rates of substance abuse, possible social isolation, and stigma (Goodman et al., 2007). Therefore, it is important to provide social support, mental health counseling, and other resources that attend to the women's multiple concerns. Reaching Out About Depression (ROAD) aims to help women living in poverty feel less isolated and more a part of the community through peer support and political action activities, hence reducing depression (Fels Smyth, Goodman, & Glenn, 2006; Goodman et al., 2007).

The ROAD program originated from the Kitchen Table Project, a support group for low-income women, where women could voice the struggles they face with others facing similar hardships (Fels Smyth et al., 2006; Goodman et al., 2007). The program uses peer support through "supportive action workshops," where graduates of the workshops facilitate a group open to the community on different topics, such as economic inequality, intimate partner violence, motherhood, and depression. One of the activities of the group is to plan an action event to raise awareness of depression and poverty in the community (Goodman et al., 2007). This event not only benefits the community but also helps alleviate feelings of depression in the participants by reducing feelings of helplessness and promoting leadership roles, group support, and giving the participants a voice in the community.

ROAD also provides a resource team of counseling and law school students and advocates to assist the participants with legal issues (Fels Smyth et al., 2006; Goodman et al., 2007). By giving the participants knowledge and tools to create change within their community, ROAD empowers women and facilitates consciousness-raising related to social, political, and historical systems from which the participants' difficult experiences originate (Fels Smyth et al., 2006). Focus groups and interviews with the participants have indicated that the women experienced reduced levels of depression and a higher sense of empowerment (Fels Smyth et al., 2006; Goodman, Glenn, Bohlig, Banyard, & Borges, 2009). The women also reported that, due to the community collaborations, they have increased knowledge of how to seek resources such as loans, mental health services, substance abuse programs, and career or higher education opportunities (Fels Smyth et al., 2006; Goodman et al., 2009). Last, evaluation results indicated that the advocacy approach utilized by the Resource Team allowed the women to feel less stigmatized, validated their experiences, and helped them realize that their goals were possible (Fels Smyth et al., 2006; Goodman et al., 2009). For more information about ROAD, see http://www.reachingoutaboutdepression.org/.

Strengths, Prevention, Empowerment, and Community Project

An example of a prevention approach that has as its primary focus the promotion of social change is the Strengths, Prevention, Empowerment, and Community Project (SPEC). The SPEC action research and organizational change project works collaboratively with human service organizations, such as United Way, to provide human services personnel with knowledge, tools, and experience to examine their organization's beliefs, structures, and functions. Participating organizations in SPEC acquire skills to evaluate the SPEC profile of their organizations, to change organizational practices, and to sustain the innovation. The ultimate goal of this process of reflection is to shift the emphasis in human services organizations from crisis management to the promotion of a culture of prevention. SPEC staff partner with agency personnel in transformation teams, with the aim of changing their organizations to ones that implement strength-based, preventive, empowering, and community-based approaches (Evans et al., 2011).

To promote well-being at the personal, relational, and collective levels, SPEC implements policies and practices in community settings across four domains: (1) temporal, (2) ecological, (3) participation, and (4) capabilities (Prilleltensky, 2005). *Temporal* refers to the timing of the intervention, reactive versus proactive. The *ecological* domain refers to meeting the goal of enhancing personal wellness through addressing root causes of problems, creating systems that increase community participation, removing barriers to services and supports, and endorsing social policies that enhance well-being (Prilleltensky, 2005). The *participation* domain refers to involving and empowering the people of the community to have both a "choice and a voice" in making decisions for the programs and social policies (Prilleltensky, 2005). Last, the *capabilities* domain encourages the building of competencies and utilizing of skills in an engaging and ethical way (Prilleltensky, 2005).

Evans, Hanlin, and Prilleltensky's (2007) case study illustrates the SPEC model by detailing the process of changing the salient values, beliefs and assumptions, and practices of an existing program to be more community oriented and empowerment and strength focused by using a preventative approach. For example, as SPEC guided the organization toward the goals of primary prevention, empowerment, participation, and changing community conditions, the program's employees became highly motivated toward change (Evans et al., 2007). Including employee participation in developing new principles and philosophies for the program in a collaborative process was also found to be powerful and rewarding for the program's employees (Evans et al., 2007). However, implementing new structures within the program proved to be more difficult, and SPEC project leaders faced some resistance. Evans et al. noted that learning through this experience showed how important it is to institute clear and detailed expectations for collaboration and partnership earlier in the process to avoid conflict. For example, since SPEC staff were "guests" lacking a formal agreement, they were unable to point out shortcomings in the change process. Although there are many struggles with changing an already existing program's internal framework to become more effective, Evans et al. (2007) demonstrate that SPEC has the potential to create systemic organizational change. To find out more about the SPEC project, visit http://www.specway.org/.

Activity

Describe a crisis or disaster that has occurred in your community in recent years. How has the community responded to the crisis to reduce or prevent a reoccurrence of the crisis in the future?

6 Ethical and Professional Issues in Prevention

Ethics is nothing else than reverence for life.

—Albert Schweitzer (Barsam, 2008)

Prevention is distinct from psychologists' and other human services providers' other professional activities (i.e., individual and family therapy, consultation, and assessment) and, therefore, points to the need to address unique ethical issues (Schwartz, Hage, & Gonzalez, 2012). The ethical codes of major mental health organizations stop short of addressing the unique ethical issues raised in prevention (e.g., APA, 2010). Perhaps most important, prevention targets groups of people (e.g., communities, high-risk populations, schools) and often attempts to create change, as exemplified by the SPEC project, not only in individuals but also in the multiple systems in which people interact (Trickett, 1998). Hence, preventative interventions affect and have implications not just for individuals but for all people they come in contact with within their ecological systems. This broad-scale impact leads to challenging ethical issues, such as protecting and promoting the autonomy of communities of participants.

Due to the nature of prevention interventions, ethical practice dictates the need to involve the target population or community in every stage of the prevention process, including the processes of planning, implementing, monitoring, and evaluating (Nation et al., 2003; Weissberg, Kumpfer, & Seligman, 2003). Also, as noted above, there is mounting evidence that for prevention interventions to be successful, they must be adapted to the specific context in which they will be implemented, and prevention specialists must avoid imposing their own values on a community (Durlak, 2003; McIntosh, Jason, Robinson, & Brzezinski, 2004; Nation et al., 2003; Vera & Reese, 2000; Weissberg et al., 2003). The participation of community leaders, members, and service providers (e.g., counselors, teachers) not only protects against the imposition of practitioners' values but also facilitates the fit of the intervention with the specific community context (Nation et al., 2003;

Weissberg et al., 2003). Since it is important that prevention programs are well supported over time (Reiss & Price, 1996; Vera & Reese, 2000), another reason for practitioners to collaborate with the community is to ensure that the prevention programs are sustained.

Informed Consent

An additional and related issue in conducting prevention interventions is obtaining informed consent, which is a central issue in ethical practice to ensure truly autonomous participation. This process of obtaining informed consent is more challenging in prevention work that typically affects multiple individuals and systems. For example, unique to work in prevention is often the lack of a clearly defined client (Bloom, 1996; Pope, 1990), which can complicate the design of the informed consent process. For example, informed consent is a different process when it needs to be obtained for a prevention intervention at a school that will affect all the children at the school, their families, and potentially their community.

Also, unlike traditional therapeutic interventions, preventive interventions often not only involve a large group of participants but also typically serve those who are not actively seeking services (Conyne, 2004). So prevention interventions are often provided in a setting (e.g., community agency) without active consent from the participants. The imposed nature of the intervention has the potential of exacerbating the existing power imbalance between practitioners or researchers and participants as the prevention practitioner is viewed as acting with expertise and authority to address a problem (Trickett, 1998). Hence, the typical informed consent process for establishing a therapeutic relationship with a client cannot be followed. As a result, the question of obtaining appropriate consent from all stakeholders when engaging in prevention is critical, and procedures to ensure the dignity and autonomy with respect to decisions about participation are paramount (Goodman et al., 2004).

Confidentiality

The use of a group or community as participants in prevention work can also complicate the process of maintaining confidentiality (Bloom, 1996; Pope, 1990). Rather than having one confidentiality agreement between the practitioner and client, prevention denotes multiple individuals receiving the intervention and often multiple individuals involved in service delivery. Potentially exacerbating these confidentiality issues is the fact that prevention topics often involve sensitive issues and materials (e.g., substance use and abuse, HIV/AIDS, family violence). Hence, some interventions, particularly those that target high-risk groups, may involve stigma related to participation (Offord, Kraemer, Kazdin, Jensen, & Harrington, 1998). Thus, participating in a prevention intervention denotes a risk to confidentiality. For example, a prevention intervention that trains school psychologists to intervene with children who are at a high risk for dropout because of poor grades poses multiple risks for confidentiality. To identify the children who are at high risk as well as potentially separating those students to intervene connotes risks to confidentiality. Hence, ethical practice requires that practitioners and researchers adequately convey potential risks of confidentiality to participants as they make a decision about whether or not to participate, as well as to take feasible steps to protect participants' confidentiality. For example, intervention meeting times can be scheduled after school or at a place where other students are meeting for other group activities.

In addition, unlike individual therapy, understanding potential benefits and harm is more complicated in prevention work. Due to the possibility of both direct and indirect harm and the complications inherent in preventive interventions, issues of informed consent are important throughout the process of an intervention. Unforeseen results may become apparent during the course of an intervention (Durlak & Wells, 1997), and unique ethical issues are often raised in evaluating prevention programs. For example, some programs have either not been effective or have resulted in an unwanted increase in the target behavior one is attempting to change or reduce (Lynam et al., 1999).

Evaluation

Finally, since preventive interventions affect not only the individual but also the individual's immediate system and larger community (Albee, 1986; Durlak & Wells, 1997), evaluation issues are complicated, and prevention interventions often involve greater potential for negative outcomes. A prevention program often attempts to not only educate and create awareness and/or behavior change in members of a community but also affect environmental and cultural change in the community. As a result, a change in behavior in an individual could have unforeseen results on that individual's family or community.

Additionally, prevention researchers must be competent in a variety of methods to evaluate multiple ecological levels. Examples of specific approaches to evaluation in prevention include needs assessment, formative and summative evaluation, and long-term follow-up (Romano & Hage, 2000a). For example, evaluation of a prevention program that only focuses on one ecological level (e.g., individual), may only assess gains in knowledge (not behavior change), leading to an incomplete assessment. Furthermore, conducting an evaluation immediately after the intervention, with no further follow-up, may create misleading results. Finally, prevention interventions that focus on social change often do not fit within traditional methods of quantitative research (Prilleltensky & Nelson, 2009). To understand the subjective and contextual experience of the participant necessitates knowledge of qualitative methods.

In sum, core differences exist between prevention and treatment, such as the systemic focus and large-scale target population, as well as specific differences, such as confidentiality issues in secondary prevention. In prevention, an effort needs to be made to protect the autonomy and rights of both the individual and the community. Finally, further work is needed to develop guidance in addressing ethical issues in prevention work, such as developing a set of ethical guidelines that directly addresses ecological systems and cultural context and promotes social justice. Some questions that remain include (a) What are the best approaches to ensure autonomous participation of all those affected by prevention interventions? (b) How can a prevention practitioner ensure confidentiality of those trained to provide the interventions? (c) What are the best methods to assess sustainable results at multiple ecological levels? (d) What is the best method to include participants in interpreting results? In sum, the ultimate goal is to prepare prevention practitioners and researchers who are competent in addressing the ethical issues that are raised in prevention work.

Prevention Program Dissemination and Stakeholders

One of the final steps in prevention best practices is regular dissemination of information about the prevention program throughout the duration of the program, as well as at the conclusion of the program. Ideally, after final data are collected, analyzed, and reviewed with stakeholders and policy makers, the information will be used to develop the next stage of the prevention initiative. Stages of information dissemination begin with announcements of the prevention initiative, after agreements to begin the prevention program have been reached with key stakeholders. Who receives the announcements will depend on the type of program offered and where it is offered. For example, in schools, parents and guardians, school personnel, and community stakeholders are important constituents to receive regular communication. Depending on age and nature of the prevention program, all students in the school may also be informed. As another example, a health care–based prevention program that encourages health professionals to assess teens for risk behaviors (e.g., smoking, sexual activity, and alcohol use) would be announced to all clinic staff, parents, and guardians. Announcements can be made through group meetings, newsletters, electronic messages via personal social media, and local media outlets. Details about the program, people involved, and start and end dates are best announced through these communication vehicles. A specific contact person or persons should be identified who can receive questions and comments about the program. Once the program has been implemented, regular reports about the program should be disseminated, such as when the program begins, at midpoint, and at the conclusion. These contacts with stakeholders can be also used for collection of process-evaluative data (e.g., Do you know about the program? What have you heard? How has the program affected you?).

At the conclusion of the program, major dissemination of findings must be conducted with stakeholders and the professional community. Similar to the start of the program, dissemination is best done through several outlets (e.g., in person, social media, etc.). In addition, the prevention specialist should prepare a formal presentation of the program and evaluative and/or research results through professional outlets, such as at conferences and in manuscripts for publication. It is important that dissemination about the prevention program and the data gathered from it be presented in language and format that is suitable to the audience. A highly technical and statistical report may not be as informative to community stakeholders as one that describes the prevention program and emphasizes qualitative outcomes rather than highly sophisticated statistical data. However, professional journal publication may demand more sophisticated analyses, either quantitative or qualitative, depending on the journal.

In addition to information about the program that just ended, stakeholders should use the information gained from this program to plan for ways to continue to offer prevention programs that address the particular issue. Seldom, if ever, will one isolated program that is delivered for a period of time inoculate all recipients against the problem behavior or promote positive behaviors without revisiting the issue. In this chapter, we have written about how prevention and health promotion must be addressed from several perspectives and that issues faced by individuals as well as larger groups often require long-term commitment to change and continued monitoring. Therefore, part of the dissemination process must be a review of the completed prevention program and dialogue about how best to continue addressing the issue, either through prevention of behaviors, promotion of health-enhancing behaviors, and/changes in public policy. As an example, a school-based drug and alcohol prevention program will require that components of the program be delivered throughout the years of schooling. The components of the program will obviously be adapted to be age appropriate, but the objectives can be similar, that is, to prevent student and alcohol use, especially as students get older and have easier access to alcohol and drugs. Therefore, the end of one prevention program and discussion of the results can be used to spur the next version of the program. Results of the earlier program can be used to help develop an improved version. However, dialogue with key stakeholders must occur. Historically, prevention programs have often been implemented after a tragedy occurs, such as an alcohol-related death, a drug overdose, school violence, or a suicide resulting from cyber-bullying. While developing such programs is positive, too often they are developed quickly and without strong theoretical foundations. An ongoing dialogue with community stakeholders can help keep the focus on preventing problems and fostering positive and proactive behaviors and avoid the tendency to quickly develop a program after a crisis, without thoughtful consultation and dialogue.

Funding and Resources for Prevention

This book as well as the entire series in the *Prevention Practice Kit* provides information and strategies to advance prevention practices in varying settings and population groups. However, a question that is often raised is how to learn about and secure additional resources and funding for prevention practices and initiatives. The question can be addressed in different ways, depending on the setting, clientele, and stakeholders. For example, school counselors who want more information about resources for prevention of school bullying can review national registries as discussed above for model programs and also access information through U.S. Government agencies such as the Centers for Disease Control and Prevention (CDC). Other sources of information are state departments of education, health, and human services, which can direct counselors to local model programs. Access to electronic information greatly increases the amount of information that is available to human development specialists.

In addition to identifying information about model prevention programs, another major issue is securing funding for prevention within a local setting, such as a school or community center. Realistically, human development professionals who deliver primary services do not have much additional time to identify sources of funding, and even less time for writing time-consuming grants for prevention. Therefore, they need to be creative in delivering prevention within their setting without incurring much additional costs. In fact, a commitment to prevention may be more cost-effective over a longer period compared with focusing on remediation and crisis intervention. For example, a school-based prevention program designed to ease the transition of students moving from middle to high school may reduce the amount of time that counselors and school staff spend with individual students once they enroll in high school. In these types of settings, an important place to start is with key stakeholders who can provide information and support for the prevention initiative. In addition to commitment and emotional support, stakeholders can also suggest, and perhaps approve, a reallocation of the professionals' time to work on a prevention project. In the case of schools, the district may provide additional funding for school personnel to work on prevention initiatives during the summer. State departments of education, health, and human services often receive grant funds from U.S. government entities and private foundations to advance prevention. In recent years, such funds have been allocated for antibullying programs in the schools and programs to reduce the incidence of obesity and diabetes in communities. A very important component of this avenue to secure additional resources is to involve key stakeholders to ensure that an important issue is being addressed and that stakeholders are supportive.

Another avenue to pursue potential funding sources is to investigate the feasibility of practitioners partnering with other institutions and groups in the community to advance a prevention project. In the case of local communities that include a nearby college or university, faculty and research staff at the college or university may welcome community partners to collaborate on a prevention project. In these types of collaborations, universities may have secured funding for an applied prevention research project and look to identify community practitioners as partners. One way to identify university faculty and researchers who are engaged in prevention scholarship is to search university departmental websites to identify people with similar interests.

Depending on the size of the prevention grant, community practitioners may be able to receive funding for their setting to partner with a higher education institution. Since prevention is a multidisciplinary field, several departments may be engaged in prevention research, including education, public health, medicine, kinesiology, social work, and psychology. Therefore, prevention practitioners can enhance their potential to develop and implement prevention by developing prevention networks within their community. Some communities may have professional organizations of prevention specialists, such as specialists who work in addictions and chemical health or organizations like the *Minnesota Prevention Resource Center* (www.emprc.org). To locate such networks, prevention specialists may need to move beyond their major professional groups and organizations since prevention is an inter- and a multidisciplinary specialty.

Romano and Hage (2000b) identified several potential funding sources for prevention research and application projects. Their list includes federal and state agencies that have funded prevention, such as the CDC and the federal department of education. However, as previously noted, school- and community-based prevention practitioners may not have the time, resources, or inclination to research and apply for these funding streams, primarily because these grants are often large and involve multiple sites and partners. Therefore, as suggested above, becoming partners in a grant application that is developed and submitted by another larger institution may be preferable. Furthermore, larger entities, such as universities and school district offices usually have infrastructures in place for external grant development. Larger organizations often employ grant specialists who are alert to funding opportunities at the local, state, and federal levels. Therefore, becoming acquainted with grant specialists within your community and within your institution, for example, school district or health department, will identify you as a prevention specialist and someone who may be interested in a future collaboration.

Activity

Identify the offices or persons within your community that may be possible partners for funding prevention projects in your setting. If you are a school employee, the district office and your state department of education are good places to start. If you are employed in a community setting, the office of local government (e.g., mayor's office) and the state department of health may be good resources. At the university level, departments of education, public health, and psychology are examples of departments. However, these are only starting points to identify potential prevention partners and collaborators.

7 Applying Prevention Learning

Five Learning Exercises

Learning Exercise 1

National Prevention Strategy (National Prevention Council, 2011)

On June 16, 2011, the National Prevention, Health Promotion, and Public Health Council announced the release of the National Prevention Strategy, a comprehensive plan that will help increase the number of Americans who are healthy at every stage of life. Go to the webpage for this plan at http://www .healthcare.gov/prevention/nphpphc/strategy/index.html, and review the four broad strategic directions and seven priority areas of the Strategy. Develop a one-page "statement" that describes your own personal reactions to how this strategy is attempting to improve the health of Americans. What surprises you when you read it? What are the strengths and limitations of the strategy? What is left out?

Learning Exercise 2

Standards of Evidence for Prevention: What Do I Think?

As you learned in this book, SPR, led by a committee of prevention scientists, unanimously approved a set of Standards of Evidence for Prevention interventions. Review each of the levels at the SPR website http://www .preventionresearch.org/advocacy/#SofE. Can you think of an example of a prevention program that exemplifies each of these three levels? What is your reaction to the standards? Write a one-page critique of the standards, noting potential strengths and weaknesses of this system.

Learning Exercise 3

Personal, Organizational, and Community Well-Being

Watch the YouTube video by Dr. Isaac Prilleltensky, Community Well Being: Socialize or Social-Lies, located at http://www.youtube.com/watch?v= WJlx8CI-rRg or go to the Specway.org website and look over the mission statement and goals of SPEC. Explain what he means by personal, organizational, and community well-being. Do you agree or disagree with the mission and goals? How would adopting this mission change the work of mental health professionals? Discuss your answers with a colleague or member of your class.

Learning Exercise 4

Risks and Protective Factors: Applying Concepts to Real-World Examples

Review the definitions of risk and protective factor provided in the book. Take a few minutes to think about your own life history or the life history of someone you know well. What might you identify as a potential risk factor? What might you identify as a potential protective factor? How did the risk factor(s) and protective factor(s) affect one another? What impact did your own social and cultural background have on how these factors affected your life or the life of someone you know? Discuss your answers with a colleague or member of your class, or write about them in a journal entry.

Learning Exercise 5

Social Justice and Prevention

The authors of the book argue that social justice is absolutely essential to engaging in the work of prevention and that mental health providers must go beyond traditional roles to act to remove complex social, political, and economic barriers faced by individuals and communities who are marginalized. What is your reaction to this assertion? Do you agree or disagree? Why or why not? If you agree, how should we be preparing counselors and other mental health providers for this work? If you disagree, what is the rationale for your position? What role, if any, should mental health professionals play in changing unjust social conditions? Formulate your reaction in a one-page statement, and share your response with a colleague or class member.

References _____

Ajzen, I. (1991). The theory of planned behavior. *Organizational Behavior and Human Decision Processes, 50,* 179–211.

Ajzen, I., & Fishbein, M. (2004). Questions raised by a reasoned action approach: Comments on Ogden (2003). *Health Psychology, 25,* 431–434.

Albee, G. W. (1959). *Mental health manpower trends.* New York, NY: Basic Books.

Albee, G. W. (1982). Preventing psychopathology and promoting human potential. *American Psychologist, 37,* 1043–1050. doi:10.1037/0003-066X.37.9.1043

Albee, G. W. (1986). Toward a just society: Lessons from observations on the primary prevention of psychopathology. *American Psychologist, 41,* 891–898.

Albee, G. W. (1987). Powerlessness, politics, and prevention: The community mental health approach. In K. Hurrelmann, F. X. Kaufmann, & F. Losel (Eds.), *Social intervention: Potential and constraints* (pp. 37–52). New York, NY: de Gruyter.

Albee, G. W. (1999). Prevention, not treatment, is the only hope. *Counselling Psychology Quarterly, 12,* 133–146.

Albee, G. W. (2000). Commentary on prevention and counseling psychology. *The Counseling Psychologist, 28,* 845–853.

Albee, G. W. (2005). Call to revolution in the prevention of emotional disorders. *Ethical Human Psychology and Psychiatry, 7,* 37–44.

American Psychological Association. (2010). *Ethical principles of psychologists and code of conduct* (2002, Amended June 1, 2010). Retrieved from http://www.apa.org/ethics/code/index.aspx

Asian/Pacific Islander Youth Violence Prevention Center. (2010). *National academic centers of excellence on youth violence prevention.* Washington, DC: Center for Disease Control and Prevention.

Bandura, A. (1986). *Social foundations of thought and action.* Englewood Cliffs, NJ: Prentice Hall.

Barsam, A. P. (2008). *Reverence for life: Albert Schweitzer's great contribution to ethical thought.* New York, NY: Oxford University Press.

Bemak, F. (2005). Reflections on multiculturalism, social justice, and empowerment groups for academic success: A critical discourse for contemporary schools. *Professional School Counseling, 8,* 401–406.

Benson, P. L. (2006). *All kids are our kids: What communities must do to raise caring and responsible children and adolescents* (2nd ed.). Minneapolis, MN: Search Institute.

Bloom, M. (1996). *Primary prevention practices.* Thousand Oaks, CA: Sage.

Bond, L. A., & Carmola Hauf, A. M. (2007). Community-based collaboration: An overarching best practice in prevention. *The Counseling Psychologist, 35,* 567–575.

Brauner, C. B., & Stephen, B. C. (2006). Estimating the prevalence of early childhood serious emotional/behavioral disorder. *Public Health Reports, 121,* 303–310.

Brown, C. H. (2011). *The International Registry of Preventive Trials, a project of the society for prevention research* [Prevention Science & Methodology Group Videos]. Retrieved from http://www.psmg.usf.edu/videos.html

Bumgarger, B., & Perkins, D. (2009). After randomized trials: Issues related to dissemination of evidence-based interventions. *Journal of Children's Services, 3,* 53–61.

Catalano, R. F., Berglund, M. L., Ryan, J. A. M., Lonczak, H. S., & Hawkins, J. D. (2002). Positive youth development in the United States: Research findings on evaluations of positive youth development programs. *Prevention & Treatment, 5,* Article 15. Retrieved from http://psycnet.apa.org/journals/pre/5/1/l

Centers for Disease Control and Prevention, National Center for Injury Prevention and Control. (2005). *Web-based injury statistics query and reporting system (WISQARS).* Retrieved from http://www.cdc.gov/injury/wisqars/index.html

Chew, W., Osseck, J., Raygor, D., Eldridge-Houser, J., & Cox, C. (2010). Developmental assets: Profile of youth in a juvenile justice facility. *Journal of School Health, 80,* 66–72.

Christopher, M. S., Skillman, G. D., Kirkhart, M. W., & D'Souza, J. B. (2006). The effect of normative and behavioral persuasion on help seeking in Thai and American college students. *Journal of Multicultural Counseling and Development, 34,* 80–93.

Coard, S. I., Foy-Watson, S., Zimmer, C., & Wallace, A. (2007). Considering culturally relevant parenting practices in intervention development and adaptation: A randomized controlled trial of the Black Parenting Strengths and Strategies (BPSS) program. *The Counseling Psychologist, 35,* 797–820.

Connell, A., Dishion, T. J., Yasui, M., & Kavanagh, K. (2007). An adaptive approach to family intervention: Linking engagement in family-centered intervention to reductions in adolescent problem behavior. *Journal of Consulting and Clinical Psychology, 75,* 568–579. doi:10.1037/0022-006X.75.4.568

Conwell, Y. (2001). Suicide in later life: A review and recommendations for prevention [Supplemental material]. *Suicide and Life Threatening Behavior, 31,* 32–47.

Conyne, R. K. (2004). *Preventive counseling: Helping people to become empowered in systems and settings* (2nd ed.). New York, NY: Brunner-Routledge.

Conyne, R. (2010). *Prevention program development and evaluation.* Thousand Oaks, CA: Sage.

Conyne, R. K., Newmeyer, M. D., Kenny, M., Romano, J. L., & Matthews, C. R. (2008). Two key strategies for teaching prevention: Specialized course and infusion. *Journal of Primary Prevention, 29,* 375–401.

Costello, E., Angold, A., Burns, B. J., Erkanli, A., Stangl, D. K., & Tweed, D. L. (1996). The Great Smoky Mountains study of youth: Functional impairment and serious emotional disturbance. *Archives of General Psychiatry, 53,* 1137–1143.

Danish, S. J. (1990). Ethical considerations in the design, implementation, and evaluation of developmental interventions. In C. B. Fisher & W. W. Tryon (Eds.), *Ethics in applied developmental psychology: Emerging issues in an emerging field: Vol. 4. Annual advances in applied developmental psychology* (pp. 93–112). Westport, CT: Greenwood Press.

Davidson, M. M., & Bowen, N. (2011). Academia meets community agency: How to foster positive collaboration in domestic violence and sexual assault work. *Journal of Family Violence, 26*, 309–318.

Durlak, J. A. (1998). Common risk and protective factors in successful prevention programs. *American Journal of Orthopsychiatry, 68*, 512–520.

Durlak, J. A. (2003). Effective prevention and health promotion programming. In T. P. Gullotta & M. Bloom (Eds.), *Encyclopedia of primary prevention and health promotion* (pp. 61–69). New York, NY: Kluwer.

Durlak, J. A., & Wells, A. M. (1997). Primary prevention mental health programs for children and adolescents: A meta-analytic review. *American Journal of Community Psychology, 25*, 115–152.

Erasmus, D. (n.d.). *BrainyQuote.com*. Retrieved from http://www.brainyquote.com/quotes/quotes/d/desiderius148997.html

Evans, S. D., Hanlin, C. E., & Prilleltensky, I. (2007). Blending ameliorative and transformative approaches in human service organizations: A case study. *Journal of Community Psychology, 35*, 329–346.

Evans, S., Prilletensky, O., McKenzie, A., Prilleltensky, I., Nogueras, D., Huggins, C., & Mescia, N. (2011). Promoting strengths, prevention, empowerment, and community change through organizational development: Lessons for research, theory, and practice. *Journal of Prevention & Intervention in the Community, 39*, 50–64. doi:10.1080/10852352.2011.530166

Fels Smyth, K., Goodman, L., & Glenn, C. (2006). The full-frame approach: A new response to marginalized women left behind by special services. *American Journal of Orthopsychiatry, 76*, 489–502.

Fishbein, M. (Ed.). (1967). *Readings in attitude theory and measurement*. New York, NY: Wiley.

Fishbein, M., & Ajzen, I. (2010). *Predicting and changing behavior: The reasoned action approach*. New York, NY: Psychology Press.

Flay, B. R., Biglan, A., Boruch, R. F., González Castro, F., Gottfredson, D., Kellam, S., . . . Ji, P. (2005). Standards of evidence: Criteria for efficacy, effectiveness and dissemination. *Prevention Science, 6*, 151–175. doi:10.1007/s11121-005-5553-y

Forehand, R. L., & Long, N. (2002). *Parenting the strong willed child: The clinically proven five-week program for parents of two- to six-year-olds*. Chicago, IL: Contemporary Books.

Goodman, L. A., Glenn, C., Bohlig, A., Banyard, V., & Borges, A. M. (2009). Feminist relational advocacy: Processes and outcomes from the perspective of low-income women with depression. *The Counseling Psychologist, 37*, 848–876.

Goodman, L. A., Liang, B., Helms, J. E., Latta, R. E., Sparks, E., & Weintraub, S. R. (2004). Training counseling psychologists as social justice agents: Feminist and multicultural principles in Action. *The Counseling Psychologist, 32*, 793–837.

Goodman, L. A., Litwin, A., Bohlig, A., Weintraub, S. R., Green, A., Walker, J., . . . Ryan, N. (2007). Applying feminist theory to community practice: A case example of a multi-level empowerment intervention for low-income women with depression. In E. Aldarando (Ed.), *Promoting social justice through mental health practice* (pp. 265–290). New York, NY: Lawrence Erlbaum.

Greenberg, M. T., Domitrovich, C., & Bumbarger, B. (2001). The prevention of mental disorders in school-aged children: Current state of the field. *Prevention & Treatment, 4*, Article 1.

Greenberg, M. T., Weissberg, R. P., O'Brien Utne, M., Zins, J. E., Fredericks, L., Resnik, H., & Elias, M. J. (2003). Enhancing school-based prevention and youth development through coordinated social, emotional, and academic learning. *American Psychologist, 58,* 466–474.

Guerrero, A. P. S., Goebert, D. A., Alicata, D. A., & Bell, C. K. (2009). Striving for a culturally responsive process in training health professionals on Asian American and Pacific Islander youth violence prevention. *Aggression and Violent Behavior, 14,* 499–505. doi:10.1016/j.avb.2009.07.011

Hage, S. M. (2005). Future considerations for fostering multicultural competence in mental health and educational settings: Social justice implications. In M. Constantine & D. W. Sue (Eds.), *Strategies for building multicultural competence in mental health and educational settings* (pp. 285–302). Hoboken, NJ: Wiley.

Hage, S. M., & Kenny, M. E. (2009). Promoting a social justice approach to prevention: Future directions for training, practice, and research. *Journal of Primary Prevention, 30,* 75–87.

Hage, S. M., Romano, J. L., Conyne, R. K., Kenny, M., Matthews, C., Schwartz, J. P., & Waldo, M. (2007). Best practices guidelines on prevention practice, research, training, and social advocacy for psychologists. *The Counseling Psychologist, 35,* 493–566.

Hartung, P. J., & Blustein, D. L. (2002). Reason, intuition, and social justice: Elaborating Parsons' career decision making model. *Journal of Counseling and Development, 80,* 41–47.

Horne, A., Bartolomucci, C., & Newman, D. (2003). *Bully busters: Bullies, victims and bystanders—A manual for elementary school teachers.* Champaign, IL: Research Press.

Israel, B., Schultz, A., Parker, E., & Becker, A. (1998). Review of community based research: Assessing partnership approaches to improve public health. *Annual Review of Public Health, 19,* 173–202.

Jordan, C. E. (2011). Building academic research centers to advance research on violence against women: An empirical foundation. *Violence Against Women, 17,* 1123–1136. doi:10.1177/1077801211419086

Kazdin, A. E., & Blase, S. L. (2011). Rebooting psychotherapy research and practice to reduce the burden of mental illness. *Perspectives on Psychological Science, 6,* 21–37.

Kenny, M. E., & Hage, S. M. (2009). The next frontier: Prevention as an instrument of social justice. *Journal of Primary Prevention, 30,* 1–10.

Kenny, M. E., Horne, A. M., Orpinas, P., & Reese, L. E. (Eds.). (2009). *Realizing social justice: The challenge of preventive interventions.* Washington, DC: American Psychological Association.

Kidd, S. A., & Kral, M. J. (2005). Practicing participatory action research. *Journal of Counseling Psychology, 52,* 187–195.

Kiselica, M. S., & Robinson, M. (2001). Bringing advocacy counseling to life: The history, issues, and human dramas of social justice work in counseling. *Journal of Counseling and Development, 79,* 387–397.

Kumper, K. L., & Summerhays, J. F. (2006). Prevention approaches to enhance resilience among high-risk youth. *Annual New York Academy of Science, 1094,* 151–163.

Lopez, S. J., & Snyder, C. R. (Eds.). (2009). *Oxford handbook of positive psychology* (2nd ed.). New York, NY: Oxford University Press.

Luthar, S. S., Cicchetti, D., & Becker, B. (2000). The construct of resilience: A critical evaluation and guidelines for future work. *Child Development, 71*, 543–562.

Lynam, D. R., Milich, R., Zimmerman, R., Novak, S. P., Logan, T. K., Martin, C., & Clayton, R. (1999). Project DARE: No effects at 10-year follow-up. *Journal of Consulting and Clinical Psychology, 67*, 590–593.

Martin, S. (2009). Roadmap for change: An APA task force previews its recommendations for transforming psychology practice to meet the demands of a new world. *Monitor on Psychology, 40, 66.*

Masten, A. S., Best, K., & Garmezy, N. (1990). Resilience and development: Contributions from the study of children who overcame adversity. *Development and Psychopathology, 2*, 425–444.

McIntosh, J. M., Jason, L. A., Robinson, W. L., & Brzezinski, L. (2004). Multiculturalism and primary prevention: Toward a new primary prevention culture. *Journal of Primary Prevention, 25*, 1–15.

Montaño, D. E., & Kasprzky, D. (2002). The theory of reasoned action and the theory of planned behavior. In K. Glanz, B. K. Rimer, & F. M. Lewis (Eds.), *Health behavior and health education: Theory, research, and practice* (pp. 67–98). San Francisco, CA: Jossey-Bass.

Morsillo, J., & Prilleltensky, I. (2007). Social action with youth: Interventions, evaluation, and psychopolitical validity. *Journal of Community Psychology, 35*, 725–740.

Mrazek, P., Biglan, A., & Hawkins, J. D. (2004). *Community-monitoring systems: Tracking and improving the well-being of America's children and adolescents.* Falls Church, VA: Society for Prevention Research. Retrieved from http://www .preventionresearch.org

Nation, M., Crusto, C., Wandersman, A., Kumpfer, K. L., Seybolt, D., Morrissey-Kane, E., & Davino, K. (2003). What works in prevention: Principles of effective prevention programs. *American Psychologist, 58*, 449–456.

National Center for Chronic Disease Prevention and Health Promotion. (2009). *The power of prevention: Chronic disease . . . the public health problem of the 21st century.* Atlanta, GA: U.S. Department of Health and Human Services.

National Prevention Council. (2011). *National prevention strategy.* Washington, DC: U.S. Department of Health and Human Services, Office of the Surgeon General.

O'Connell, M. E., Boat, T., & Warner, K. E. (Eds.). (2009). *Preventing mental, emotional, and behavioral disorders among young people: Progress and possibilities.* Washington, DC: National Academies Press.

Offord, D. R., Kraemer, H. C., Kazdin, A. E., Jensen, P. S., & Harrington, R. (1998). Lowering the burden of suffering from child psychiatric disorder: Trade-offs among clinical, targeted and universal interventions. *Journal of the American Academy of Child and Adolescent Psychiatry, 37*, 686–694.

Ogbu, J. U. (1981). Origins of human competence: A cultural-ecological perspective. *Child Development, 51*, 413–429.

Painter, J., Borba, C., Hynes, M., Mays, D., & Glanz, K. (2008). The use of theory in health behavior research from 2000–2005: A systematic review. *Annals of Behavioral Medicine, 35*, 358–362.

Perry, M., & Albee, G. W. (1994). On "The science of prevention." *American Psychologist, 49*, 1087–1088.

Pope, K. S. (1990). Identifying and implementing ethical standards for primary prevention. *Prevention in Human Services, 8*, 43–64.

President's New Freedom Commission on Mental Health. (2003). *Achieving the promise: Transforming mental health care in America.* Final Report (DHHS Pub. No. SMA-03-3832). Rockville, MD: U.S. Department of Health and Human Services.

Price, R. H., & Behrens, T. (2003). Working Pasteur's quadrant: Harnessing science and action for community change. *American Journal of Community Psychology, 31,* 219–223.

Prilleltensky, I. (2003). Understanding, resisting, and overcoming oppression: Towards psychopolitical validity. *American Journal of Community Psychology, 31,* 195–201.

Prilleltensky, I. (2005). Promoting well-being: Time for a paradigm shift in health and human services. *Scandinavian Journal of Public Health,* 33(Suppl. 66), 53–60.

Prilleltensky, I. (2012). Wellness as fairness. *American Journal of Community Psychology, 49,* 1–21.

Prilleltensky, I., & Nelson, G. (2009). Community psychology: Advancing social justice. In D. Fox, I. Prilleltensky, & A. Austin (Eds.), *Critical psychology* (2nd ed.). Thousand Oaks, CA: Sage.

Prochaska, J. O., DiClemente, C. C., & Norcross, J. C. (1992). In search of how people change: Applications to addictive behaviors. *American Psychologist, 47,* 1102–1114.

Prochaska, J. O., Evers, K. E., Prochaska, J. M., Van Marter, D., & Johnson, J. L. (2007). Efficacy and effectiveness trials: Examples from smoking cessation and bullying prevention. *Journal of Health Psychology, 12,* 170–178.

Prochaska, J. O., Johnson, S., & Lee, P. (2009). The transtheoretical model of behavior change. In S. A. Shumaker, J. K. Ockene, & K. A. Riekert (Eds.), *The handbook of behavior change* (3rd ed., pp. 59–83). New York, NY: Springer.

Reese, L. E., & Vera, E. M. (2007). Culturally relevant prevention: The scientific and practical considerations of community-based programs. *The Counseling Psychologist, 35,* 763–778.

Reiss, D., & Price, R. H. (1996). National research agenda for prevention research: The National Institute of Mental Health report. *American Psychologist, 51,* 1109–1115.

Ringel, J. S., & Sturm, R. (2001). National estimates of mental health utilization and expenditures for children in 1998. *Journal of Behavioral Health Services & Research, 28,* 319–333. doi:10.1007/BF02287247

Romano, J. L. (2013). Prevention in the 21st century. In E. Vera (Ed.), *Oxford handbook of prevention in counseling psychology.* New York, NY: Oxford University Press.

Romano, J. L., & Hage, S. M. (2000a). Prevention: A call to action. *The Counseling Psychologist, 28,* 854–856.

Romano, J. L., & Hage, S. M. (2000b). Prevention and counseling psychology: Revitalizing commitments for the 21st century. *The Counseling Psychologist, 28,* 733–763.

Romano, J. L., & Netland, J. D. (2008). The application of the theory of reasoned action and planned behavior to prevention science in counseling psychology. *The Counseling Psychologist, 36,* 777–806.

Rotheram-Borus, M., & Duan, N. (2003). Next generation of preventive interventions. *Journal of the American Academy of Child & Adolescent Psychiatry, 42,* 518–526. doi:10.1097/01.CHI.0000046836.90931.E9

Rutter, M. (1979). Protective factors in children's responses to stress and disadvantage. In M. Whalen & J. E. Rolf (Eds.), *Primary prevention of psychopathology: Vol. 3. Social competence in children* (pp. 49–74). Hanover, NH: University Press of New England.

Sanson-Fisher, R., & Turnbull, D. (1987). "To do or not to do?" Ethical problems for behavioral medicine. In S. Fairbairn & G. Fairbairn (Eds.), *Psychology, ethics and change* (pp. 191–211). New York, NY: Routledge.

Schwartz, J. P., Hage, S. M., & Gonzalez, D. (2012). A new paradigm for prevention work: The development of an ethical code. In L. Vera (Ed.). *Handbook of prevention in counseling psychology*. New York, NY: Oxford University Press.

Schwartz, J. P., & Lindley, D. L. (2009). Impacting sexism through social justice prevention: Implications at the person and environmental levels. *Journal of Primary Prevention, 30,* 27–41.

Seligman, M. E. P., Steen, T. A., Park, N., & Peterson, C. (2005). Positive psychology progress: Empirical validation of interventions. *American Psychologist, 60,* 410–421.

Snyder, C. R., & Lopez, S. J. (2007). *Positive psychology: The scientific and practical explorations of human strengths.* Thousand Oaks, CA: Sage.

Sue, D. W., & Sue, D. (2008). *Counseling the culturally different: Theory and practice* (5th ed.). Hoboken, NJ: Wiley.

Toporek, R. L., Gerstein, L. H., Fouad, N. A., Roysircar, G., & Israel, T. (2005). *Handbook of social justice in counseling psychology.* Thousand Oaks: Sage.

Toporek, R. L., Lewis, J., & Crethar, H. C. (2009). Promoting systemic change through the advocacy competencies. *Journal of Counseling and Development, 87,* 260–269.

Trickett, E. J. (1998). Toward a framework for defining and resolving ethical issues in the protection of communities involved in primary prevention projects. *Ethics & Behavior, 8,* 321–337.

Trickett, E. J., & Levin, G. B. (1990). Paradigms for prevention: Providing a context for confronting ethical issues. *Prevention in Human Services, 8,* 3–21.

Trust for America's Health. (2009). *Poll: American public supports investment in prevention as part of health care reform.* Washington, DC: Author.

Tutu, D., & Tutu, N. (2007). *The words of Desmond Tutu* (2nd ed.). New York, NY: Newmarket Press.

Umemoto, K., Baker, C. K., Helm, S., Maio, T., Goebert, D. A., & Hishinuma, E. S. (2009). Moving toward comprehensiveness and sustainability in a social ecological approach to youth violence prevention: Lessons from the Asian/Pacific Islander Youth Violence Prevention Center. *American Journal of Community Psychology, 44,* 221–232.

U.S. Department of Health and Human Services. (2003). *Prevention makes common "cents."* Washington, DC: Author.

U.S. Public Health Service, Office of the Surgeon General. (2004). *Report of the Surgeon General's Conference on Children's Mental Health: A national action agenda.* Rockville, MD: U.S. Department of Health and Human Services.

Vera, E., Buhin, L., & Isacco, A. (2009). The role of prevention in psychology's social justice agenda. In M. Kenny, A. Horne, P. Orpinas, & L. Reese (Eds.), *Realizing social justice: The challenge of prevention interventions* (pp. 79–96). Washington, DC: American Psychological Association.

Vera, E. M., & Reese, L. E. (2000). Preventive interventions with school-age youth. In S. D. Brown & R. W. Lent (Eds.), *Handbook of counseling psychology* (pp. 411–434). New York, NY: Wiley.

Vera, E. M., & Speight, S. (2007). Advocacy, outreach, and prevention: Integrating social action roles in professional training. In E. Aldarondo (Ed.), *Advancing social justice through clinical practice* (pp. 373–390). Mahwah, NJ: Lawrence Erlbaum.

Vogelzang, S. N., Kritchevsky, S. B., Beekman, A. T., Newman, A. B., Satterfield, S., Simmsick, E. M., & Penninx, B. W. (2008). Depressive symptoms and change in abdominal obesity in older persons. *Archives of General Psychiatry, 65,* 1386–1393.

Wadsworth, Y. (1998). What is participatory action research? *Action Research International,* Paper 2.

Walsh, M. E., DePaul, J., & Park-Taylor, J. (2009). Prevention as a mechanism for promoting positive development in the context of risk: Principles of best practice. In M. E. Kenny, A. M. Horne, P. Orpinas, & L. E. Reese (Eds.), *Realizing social justice: The challenge of preventive interventions* (pp. 57–78). Washington, DC: American Psychological Association.

Wandersman, A., Morrissey, E., Davino, K., Seybolt, D., Crusto, C., Nation, M., . . . Imm, P. (1998). Comprehensive quality programming and accountability: Eight essential strategies for implementing successful prevention programs. *Journal of Primary Prevention, 19,* 3–30.

Ward, J. V. (2000). *The skin we're in: Teaching our teens to be emotionally strong, socially smart and spiritually connected.* New York, NY: Simon & Schuster.

Watts, R. J. (1994). Graduate training for a diverse world. *American Journal of Community Psychology, 22,* 807–809. doi:10.1007/BF02521562

Weissberg, R. P., Kumpfer, K. L., & Seligman, M. E. P. (2003). Prevention that works for children and youth: An introduction. *American Psychologist, 58,* 425–432.

Weisz, J. R., Sandler, I. N., Durlak, J. A., & Anton, B. S. (2005). Promoting and protecting youth mental health through evidence-based prevention and treatment. *American Psychologist, 60,* 628–648.

Werner, E., & Smith, R. (1992). *Overcoming the odds: High risk children from birth to adulthood.* Ithaca, NY: Cornell University Press.

World Health Organization. (Eds.). (2011). *Global status report on noncommunicable diseases 2010: Description of the global burden of NCDs, their risk factors and determinants.* New York, NY: Author.

Index

About the Authors _____

Sally Hage is Program Director of the Counseling Psychology program in the Department of Psychology at Springfield College, Massachusetts. She is the Chair of the Prevention Section of the Society of Counseling Psychology and is a licensed psychologist and a licensed mental health counselor. She has published numerous journal articles and book chapters and given presentations in the areas of prevention, social justice, prevention of intimate partner violence, and spiritual and religious diversity. She received her PhD in counseling psychology from the University of Minnesota and her MDiv from the University of Notre Dame.

John L. Romano is a professor in the Department of Educational Psychology, Counseling and Student Personnel Psychology Program, at the University of Minnesota. He has served terms as Program Coordinator and Training Director, Department Chair, and Assistant Vice President for International Scholarship at the University of Minnesota. His research and writing in recent years have focused on prevention in the counseling, psychology, and the human development professions. He is a founding member and first Chair of the Prevention Section of the Society of Counseling Psychology and was the recipient of the Inaugural Lifetime Achievement Award given by the Prevention Section. He also has been a corecipient of the American Counseling Association Research Award. Throughout his career, he has been active internationally—serving in the Peace Corps in Nigeria, as an external examiner for institutions in Malaysia and Singapore, and as a visiting professor in Thailand. He is also cofounder of the Minnesota International Counseling Institute. He is a Fellow of the American Psychological Association, Divisions 17 (Counseling Psychology) and 52 (International Psychology). He has served on various counseling and psychology journal editorial boards at home and abroad and served two terms on the Minnesota Board of Psychology. He is licensed as a psychologist and marriage and family therapist in Minnesota.

⑤SAGE research**methods**

The essential online tool for researchers from the world's leading methods publisher

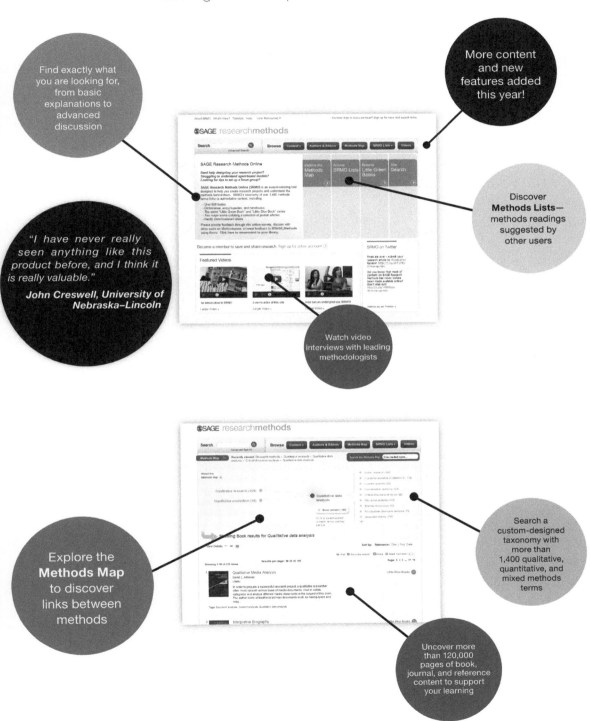

Find exactly what you are looking for, from basic explanations to advanced discussion

More content and new features added this year!

"I have never really seen anything like this product before, and I think it is really valuable."
John Creswell, University of Nebraska–Lincoln

Discover **Methods Lists**— methods readings suggested by other users

Watch video interviews with leading methodologists

Explore the **Methods Map** to discover links between methods

Search a custom-designed taxonomy with more than 1,400 qualitative, quantitative, and mixed methods terms

Uncover more than 120,000 pages of book, journal, and reference content to support your learning

Find out more at
www.sageresearchmethods.com